# HACK E-MAIL

## Connect with Anyone,
## Build your Business and Brand,
## Become an Unstoppable Force

Danny Flood

## This book is third in a series:

# Buy Your Own Island

## The Ultimate Guide to Breaking Free and Making Your Dreams Reality

**DOWNLOAD MY NEW AUDIO BOOK FOR FREE!**

To say thanks for reading this book,
I'd like to give you the audiobook for my #1 best-selling
book, "Buy Your Own Island" - 100% free!

For more resources, articles, and educational and inspirational
podcasts, visit:
**www.OpenWorldMag.com**, a magazine and podcast managed by the
author.

Also - if you enjoy the information in this guide, I'd appreciate a
review :-)
You can write one here.

# PRAISE FOR *BUY YOUR OWN ISLAND* AND OTHER BOOKS BY DANNY FLOOD

## *Buy Your Own Island*
**The Ultimate Guide to Breaking Free and Making Your Dreams Reality**

"One of my favorite books on entrepreneurship! I've read a lot of books about entrepreneurship and Danny's book is surely one of my favorites. I love how he not only covers strategies, resources and tools but also the mindset that you should have as an entrepreneur. Highly recommended!"

*- Jasper Ribbers, Amazon #1 best-selling author*

"Read this book and change your life! One of the most inspiring books I have ever read; if you want to create a new life, make money and travel the world doing it this book makes you realise just how possible that is! Everyone should read this book!"

*- Nicole Hilditch, The Roaming Renegades*

"Get out and see the world - this book will help you get there... Thrilled to see this from Danny Flood, who's been engineering his own lifestyle for years. Pick this up if what you want out of life is to experience more of this world on your own terms. Then ask yourself, what is your island?"

- Nathaniel Boyle, The Daily Travel Podcast

"Since reading Danny's book we have moved to a tropical island, grown our online e-commerce jewelry web sites and opened a retail store. We broke free and are living the dream and loving life and adventure. BYOI is a wonderful tool, take the leap of faith on your dream life and make it happen."

- Alicia Hanson, Hi Octane Jewelry

"This book is full of specific tips and information, not vague generalities. The author states he spent a year putting together this book and I believe the content speaks for itself. A must guide for entrepreneurs, lifestyle designers and digital nomads."

- Liz Marino, Amazon author

" One of the top books to reach on lifestyle design. As a fellow location independent entrepreneur who has been around the block, I learned so much from this book. And as someone who knows Danny personally, I can say he writes based on genuine and unique life experiences. It's well-written, thorough, motivational, and will get you on your way to living life on your terms."

*- Grant Weherly, Amazon #1 best-selling author*

"If you want to open your eyes to a new reality where you live the life you've always dreamed of you should stop reading my review and go read this book! Danny's words are encouraging, his methods are achievable, and his insight is far beyond his years."

*- Jon Norris, Musician*

# HACK E-MAIL

### Connect with Anyone, Build Your Business and Brand, Become an Unstoppable Force

"The book is a must reading for either freelancers or for those entrepreneurs and marketing professionals who are trying to improve their performance in email outreach. I strongly believe that this book will become my trusted companion in daily email activities and will lead me securely to new business horizons! Keep up the great work, Danny :)"

*- Gabriella Miteva*

# HACKING UPWORK

### How to Make REAL MONEY as a Freelancer

*"One word: Wow! Anyone using Upwork or who is a freelancer of any kind should really invest in the time it'll take to read this eBook. You'll avoid pitfalls and unnecessary mistakes. The author offers tips that are a little out of the box but so simple, you'll wonder why it's not common sense. Definitely get this!"*

*- Anonymous Reviewer*

# HACK YOUR MIND

### To Become Bulletproof

*"Definitely changed my outlook on my life and circumstances. As entrepreneurs, keeping a positive, healthy mindset is critical. I found the section about perception filtering the most helpful. This guide has shown me how to be more effective in pursuing goals. Highly recommended."*

*- Nathaniel Wilson*

# About the Author

Danny is an author, entrepreneur, world-traveler, rabble-rouser, friend, and lover from California.

He is the founder of OpenWorld magazine, and also hosts the OpenWorld podcast where he interviews the world's most exciting adventurers and location-independent entrepreneurs. Personally, he has started 3 location-independent businesses. During that time he also traveled to 30+ countries, and reduced his working hours to 10 per week.

For additional resources, articles, and educational podcasts, visit: **www.OpenWorldMag.com**, a magazine and podcast managed by the author.
Also connect on **Twitter,** and **Facebook.**

Printed in the United States of America

Book Design by Danny Flood

First Edition

# CONTENTS

# INTRODUCTION

Ready for a secret? E-mail is one of the most powerful marketing mediums available. It's free to use, and available to everyone. E-mail is the great equalizer that levels the playing field.

Everyone is familiar with the story of David and Goliath. Goliath is huge, his armor thick, his weapons sharp. His very presence on the battlefield commands respect. David, by contrast, is the opposite. However, he does possess one simple but very effective weapon, and it decides the outcome.

If you're a David - with limited resources - then here's the great news: e-mail marketing can be your sling.

E-mail can be a powerful medium to connect with anyone in the world, and turn you and your business in to an unstoppable force that leaves your competition in the dust.

But here's the thing: most entrepreneurs and small business mana-
gers are not using e-mail in the most effective way. Most of us use
e-mail to simply send and reply to messages, but don't see e-mail
outreach as a viable marketing option.

Instead, when it comes to marketing far too many of us imitate
Goliath: trying to fit on his shield and armor, taking up his spear and
bow... despite the fact that they are too heavy and we're not big enough for them.

Using the wrong marketing techniques can be costly: a drain on the
time, energy, and resources of a small business or startup.

Furthermore, of the entrepreneurs and businesspeople who are using
e-mail in their marketing mix, the majority are doing so in a way that
is ineffective.

Far too many of us don't understand the subtle cues of effective
e-mail communication that make effective outreach so compelling
and engaging. And it gets worse. We may fire off hundreds of poorly
written e-mails and silently wait in hopes that SOME positive response will trickle back... but all too often it never does.

These days there are far too many mass untargeted mailings which get filed into the Spam folder, and long Shakespearean soliloquies that never get read.

Probably not the best way to go about it.

E-mail can be the sling, but if we're not trained in its proper use it and can backfire and end up smacking us in the face. Ouch!

I will tell you this: if you know how to write killer e-mails and can install an efficient procedure for e-mail outreach it can make promoting you and your business ridiculously easy. You can use this powerful medium to connect with anyone in the world, and turn you and your business in to an unstoppable force that leaves your competition in the dust.

## Who Am I and Why Should You Listen?

I've founded three startups, including an agency and a membership website. Now I run a blog, online magazine, podcast, and have self-published several books, including this one. E-mail outreach is the bread and butter of what I do. I have to constantly book guests, interview people, promote content and products, find affiliates, and garner exposure for our brands. Within one month, I used a focused e-mail outreach campaign to increase the traffic to my blog by approximately 400% between March and April 2015.

I've also used e-mail to acquire new coaching clients, freelance clients, affiliate partners; as well as sell books, digital products, and productized services.

Equally important, I've built up a network of top achievers and movers and shakers around the world and done it all just by typing a few sentences in to my keyboard and clicking "Send." Connecting with influential people through e-mail is something that I do every single day.

When I published my first book, I used my e-mail strategy to book between 30-40 interviews for podcasts, local and online media, and more; which led a ton of exposure, sales, and subscribers. I used this successful strategy to earn features in magazines, newspapers, and radio shows across the United States - from New Orleans to Maryland.

A few minutes and a quick e-mail makes it all possible.

If I didn't understand how to use e-mail to promote my brand and business, very few people would know me or my work and I could very well be off working as an English teacher somewhere.

If you'll permit me, I want to share with you the best of what I've learned as a result of these experiences so that you too can forge ahead and bring your unique gifts to the world.

## The Power of One

Given the relationships that I've developed, people often seem to think that I have a team of virtual assistants who are always e-mailing people, establishing relationships, and building partnerships.

The truth is, I have been running and managing my current business solo. I could outsource my work, but I've endeavoured hard to find ways to build leverage into the business. **Leverage allows me to accomplish the work of five in half the time.**

Leveraging our time enables us to achieve greater and greater results, and at the forefront of leverage (where it applies to business) is e-mail communication. E-mail is perhaps the most efficient and cost-effective way to market and promote your business and brand.

It is the best medium for reaching out to new business contacts because it's low pressure and non-intrusive. E-mail allows someone to respond at a time at their convenience. It's low pressure, unlike the telephone. For reasons like these e-mail is, by far, the best way to get your foot in the door with someone.

I've tried and tested a bunch of different ways to market myself, my products, and my services, and email kicks the crap out of everything else. Nothing else out there can compare to the ease, accessibility, and sheer connecting power of e-mail.

When we take the most powerful medium and apply powerful principles of leverage, we can become a devastating force.

How you use this power is up to you.

The focus of this book is how to build leverage through effective communication cues, shortcuts, apps, and efficient procedures using e-mail.

Anyone with a computer and an internet connection can apply the strategies in this book - and the best part is, it's all completely free.

Are you ready to learn some new techniques to become an unstoppable force?

If you're alone right now, say "Hell, Yeah!" (if you're in a public place you can postpone the "hell, yeah" until later...)

It's time to finally get the attention and publicity that you deserve.

Here's my promise to you: my objective with this guide is to teach you the most powerful e-mail tools, tactics, and strategies so that you can turn e-mail into a powerful method for generating more partnerships and deals, and growing your business.

Much of this is based on tried-and-true psychology: neuro linguistic -processing (NLP), sales psychology, and direct marketing. Many of these techniques have been deployed, tested, and refined over time - and proven again and again, to deliver results.

For example: direct marketers have learnt from repeated tests that an e-mail signature in blue ink is considered to be more prestigious than one in black!

A simple color change in the signature of a letter has consistently proven, time and again, to significantly increase response rates. It's a substantial enough improvement that direct marketers are willing to pay the extra cost for a color prints versus one in black and white.

Since e-mail is at its essence simply one human communicating to another, everything that applies to NLP, direct marketing, and psychology also applies to the medium.

Through the use of subtle tweaks, you can write devastatingly persuasive e-mails that get the responses you seek. When you combine the technological prowess and cost-effectiveness of e-mail, you have at your disposable the most powerful medium of communication ever available.

## Your Mindset From This Point Forward

To succeed with any of the e-mail outreach strategies in this book,

**take up the mindset of a marketer.**

Too many entrepreneurs and self-employed people spend far too much time doing whatever trade it is that they're skilled in, and push marketing on to the backburner. Writers want to write. Designers want to design. Search engine specialists want to optimize websites for search and generate backlinks.

A marketer, on the other hand, does not dip one toe in to the marketing side of the business or outsource marketing to a virtual assistant.

**Marketing is a full-time thing.** It's not a some-of-the-time thing. It takes consistency and discipline. To succeed, you have to determine what type of metrics are most important for your business at the moment and set certain goals.

What are you hoping to get from your e-mail outreach? Do you want to find mentors and gain a foot in to a new industry? Do you want to book interviews to promote your new book? Do you want more clients for your services? Do you want to take on affiliates to promote your product? Do you want to convert one-time customers and past customers to retainer clients?

E-mail is the best medium to help you achieve all of these business objectives and more. But first you have to get clear on what are the most important metrics for your business at the moment. Then set a reasonable target - such as increasing that metric by 20% each month.

The key is to look at your campaign objectively and as a means to an end to reach your goals. This is the way a marketer approaches a campaign. Marketing needs to be a full-time, ongoing activity in order to work. A blogger who spends 95% of their time writing content and only 5% marketing their content will struggle for a long time and likely give up. A blogger who spends 40% of their time writing content and 60% marketing their content will build an audience of loyal readers and fans over time, and discover new ways to bring more value to their audience.

This advice might seem obvious at first glance, but entrepreneurs and startups are very busy and with all of the things we have to do it's easy to become lost in a forest of trees without being clear which path leads forward. Without an objective, metric-driven outlook we can easily become like the dwarves from "The Hobbit," lost within the Mirkwood, talented warriors and well-intentioned but led astray.

To drive this point home, let's draw a metaphor from another space: fitness. If you walk in to most gyms, chances are you'll see a majority of people wasting their time. Instead of working out, they're typing on their phones, checking themselves out in the mirror, or shooting around furtive glances out at other people.

Don't be the type of business owner, freelancer, entrepreneur, or self-employed person who sits around in the gym wasting time playing Candy Crush on your phone. Know what your goals are, be 100% focused from the moment you step in to the gym, and do the hard work that it takes.

Leave it all in the gym. Know what your goal is, and commit to it. Don't start e-mailing people if you're unfocused or unclear on what you're really after. Gain clarity first, then align your efforts to follow.

To succeed at anything (from weightlifting to marketing) you have to enjoy what you do, you have to commit, and you have to have clear, specific goals that are easy to reach.

Set a reasonable goal for yourself - such as contacting ten new people every Monday. Test everything in this book - from the apps to the subject lines. After a few weeks, take note of what works, and document it. Create a step-by-step process that becomes your standard operating procedure.

Tweak, optimize, and iterate, and most importantly keep practicing to gain firsthand experience on the frontlines. There's no limit to how good you can be.

## What to Expect from This Book

**This guide is broken down into five parts:**

**First, is the introduction** (that's the part you're reading now!).

**In the second chapter,** we'll cover the persuasion and influence techniques that will make it possible for you to reach out to anyone - CEOs, celebrities, press, and so on - and get the response you seek.

We'll start by dissecting what bad outreach looks like, with several examples of each. We'll pick apart the specific mistakes that doomed each interaction so that you can avoid them. Then we'll discuss a collection of specific strategies to write the most persuasive messages possible.

**Part Three** presents more than a dozen apps and strategies for making e-mail more productive, prettier, more persuasive, and more powerful. You'll learn which tools to use to dramatically decrease the amount of time you spend with e-mail, and how to make your e-mails look more professional.

I'll also share the specific strategy I use for getting through the daily e-mail crush in less than half the time, and my favorite tool for following up with new connections, partners, and leads.

**Part Four** is for hardcore e-mail hackers who want to take everything to the next level by using my favorite CRM (Client Relationship Management) app, Streak. Streak is a free add-on for Gmail which gives you superpowers when it comes to e-mail marketing. It's been my secret weapon for promoting my online business, scaling it up, and making it seem much larger than it is (I'm a one-man operation, but from the outside people regularly assume I have an entire team working for me).

**Part Five** introduces some unconventional (but very effective) strategies to find the people we want to connect with! You'll learn how to spy on competitors, and see who they interact with. You'll learn how to automate the process of discovering new e-mail addresses. You'll learn unorthodox techniques that few know about and even fewer are using. This may be the most fun chapter in the whole book.

**Part Six** features a case study from veteran e-mail "sensei" who is actively putting the power of outreach e-mail to devastating effect in his campaigns. You'll hear his story, how he did it, and some of the exact scripts and tools that he's used.

In the final pages of this book you'll find the conclusion and an appendix of all of the resources (with links) mentioned in this book.

Are you ready to enter the dojo of e-mail hacking and become a certified master? Proceed forward to chapter two, and let's get started.

# WHAT AWESOME E-MAIL OUTREACH LOOKS LIKE

Here, we'll break down the core techniques and shine light upon the dark arts of killer e-mail marketing outreach.

By now, you know that the easiest way to build your business and create powerful connections is by using e-mail.

So... how to get started?

That's what I'm going to show you in this chapter. We're going to dot the i's, cross the t's, and *break down every single component* to help you become a master communicator through e-mail in no time at all.

But before we dive in and break down to how to craft awesome e-mails that get a response, I first want to give some examples of some horrible outreach e-mails.

It's important to know what NOT to do and provide a backdrop for an alternative approach and what to focus on instead. In each example I'm going to point out what the person did wrong in each instance, and how to improve upon these common, overlooked mistakes.

I don't mean to pick on these people, and they all seem like decent folks. I would love to help them, but as you'll see, their cold messages so poorly written that I'm not even sure how or what I can do for them (besides suggesting that they read this book - hehe).

The key to remember is: the vast majority of people - perhaps 90% - are conducting e-mail outreach poorly. This equals a HUGE opportunity for those with the ability to do it the right way, using the communication techniques presented in the latter half of this chapter.

## Four Real Examples of Bad Outreach

I'm not even sure where to begin. Again, I'm sure that this guy is a decent person. However this is the first e-mail I've ever received from to Danny ▾

Hi Danny,

firstly thanks for your book - a great listen and very inspiring! (i first learnt about you from e on fire!)

In fact it further concreted our plans to create our travel video series called ▧▧▧ ▧▧▧ ▧▧▧
It is an innovative and fun (and anything but boring like most travel shows) travel series following the worldwide adventures of
Enya, a 5 year old as she travels on her scooter to the most epic locations on earth.

It is our quest to both show our daughter on the wonderful returns from foreign travel but also to show other parents that can be
fun and should be an integral part of everyones education.

the site will be on line in early May along with our first episodes from our travels in Vietnam. (We are currently filming in Vietnam !
)

Anyhow to my question : As the site / and videos will not be online before the end of April / start of May can we nominate ▧▧ ▧▧
▧▧▧ ? based on the fact that she/we would not really be 'judgable' until May time ?

Many thanks and keep up the great work !


Tnx
▧▧▧

him, and given the way it is written, it does not make a good first

impression.


Incorrect capitalization, punctuation errors... and a general "stre-

am-of-consciousness" style of rambling. I have to navigate through

several disorganized blocks of text before arriving at the purpose of

the e-mail.


The icing on the cake is the way that the e-mail is signed off: "Tnx."

Never, ever sign off your e-mails this way. I will repeat again: "Never,

ever!" Addressing your recipient the way an eighth-grader would is no

way to curry favor or have your requests be accepted.


I did respond to this e-mail, because he has read my book and he's

also a member of my e-mail list. No one ever wants to upset their e-mail subscribers or blog readers, because those are the primary source of leads and clientele for an online entrepreneur.

But when you reach out to someone, please take the time to compose a more structurally and technically sound e-mail than the one in the example above.

In this example, the sender didn't even care to distinguish my gender. Not a good start. She sent her message via Facebook (which, incidentally made it to my "Other" folder - almost guaranteeing that the vast majority of her e-mails are not even getting through), which starts: "Dear Sir/Madam."

2/26, 5:13pm

Dear Sir/Madam,

We are students from International Lifestyle Studies in Tilburg in the Netherlands. Our study is based on trendwatching and concept-development. At this moment we are in our second year and we are starting up our own company called JIB. Our assignment is to realize a product which is innovative, inspiring and creative.

During the startup of we chose the mentality group Global Lifestylers/global nomads and after a lot of group surveys, interviews and feedback we've designed a product that will fit their needs. We're very proud to present you: 'Piece of me'.

Our product is designed for global lifestyles who are traveling in between different places and who will have to create their own home all around the world. With this product we want to improve the quality of life of global lifestylers.

We would love to hear your feedback and tips. Don't hesitate to be critical: we'll only learn from that.

We would like to hear from you!
I you have any interest, please let us know we will send you our visuals

Kind regards,

JIB
- Sailing the desert, home is where the anchor drops -

Implying that someone is so androgynous that you can't even distinguish their gender is never a good way to start. Imagine if you approached a stranger in real life and told them: "Dear Sir or Madam." It probably wouldn't turn out very well.

Then the message continues into some long, rambling e-mail (TLDR). I have no idea what her product is, she has no idea who I am, and she asks me for general feedback rather than anything specific, which is far too time and effort consuming for me to want to bother.

The e-mail is all about her and provides no benefit to me whatsoever, and rather takes from me in the time to read her message and/or fulfill whatever request she is asking me to fulfill.

The most important lesson: think of e-mail as a form of communication that mimics real life. If you approached a stranger in person, you wouldn't address them as "Dear Sir or Madam..." Instead you might say something like "Hey, how's it going?" Cool, calm, and casual. You know, the way normal humans talk.

*Takeaway:* Don't impersonate a robot. Keep your e-mail personable and be **human.**

Hello. I'm interested in pursuing the nomadic lifestyle and moving to Chiang Mai. I've been building a steady client list for work. But I've also been looking into purchasing the Drop ship lifestyle by Anton Kraly. Do you have any experience with that? Any recommendations?

Thanks for your time

To his credit, this guy talks the talk, using language and terms that are specific to the topic he's talking about, and his message is refreshingly short. It reads clearly.

Unfortunately, there is no way I can respond to his request, because it does nothing for me but create extra work for me...

I have no idea how this guy found me, or why he is even e-mailing me. He placed the burden on me to figure out *how* I'm supposed to be able to help him.

If he took five minutes to search my blog he would know that I'm not a drop shipper. His request for information: "I've also been looking to purchasing the Drop ship lifestyle by Anton Kraly. Do you have any experience with that?" could be answered in five minutes with a simple Google search.

There is no mention of my work, or indeed anything meant to form a relationship with the actual person whom he's sending the message to on the other end. By making such a vague request, he is creating too much extra work for me to respond.

Moreover, he also sent me the message via Facebook, and his message ended up in my "Other" folder, just as in the example above. I didn't even see his message until weeks after it was sent, and by then it was far too late to reply.

This guy seems like a great person, and he displays in the initial paragraph that he's familiar with what I do. But this request is just awful, moreover he puts the onus on me to try to figure out how I am supposed to help him. Even worse, his repeated use of the superlative "amazing" comes across as superficial and annoying.

Hey Danny,

It was really awesome hearing your story, your interview at Entrepreneur on Fire. I resonated with so many things you said, from 'I'm weird' YES I AM! to the Eric Hoffer quote. Am-AZING!

I'm a newly starting entrepreneur, working on my website healthcut.com which I'll be launching soon, professionally an application programmer but more of a fired up business and idea generating machine.
I live in Pakistan, people here are filled with ideas and want to do something but much of that is left in talks.

I'm a person who wants to do something amazing, is there somehow you can help me? guide me? or connect me to the 'network' of amazing people like you.

awaiting reply.

Regards
^.^

The request reads:

"I'm a person who wants to do something amazing, is there somehow you can help me? guide me? or connect me to the 'network' of amazing people like you."

Yes - there is a way I can help you. Read my damn book.

# 7 Mistakes of Horrible Outreach and How to Fix Them

We were able to identify several mistakes in the examples above, which more or less doomed each message to failure in advance.

Here's a summary of the mistakes in these examples and how to fix them:

**1. Make absolutely certain that your e-mail is structurally and technically sound.** Since your initial e-mail is the first impression the other person has of you, is it a terrible idea to send a message full of incorrect punctuation and capitalization errors. As the saying goes, "you never get a second chance to make a good first impression," and given the influx of e-mail we all get, and the close proximity of the "Delete" button, it's never been more true than in e-mail communication.

**2. Keep it colloquial, and customize for the recipient.** Never start an e-mail with "Dear Sir/Madam." It's impossible not to cringe when you see those words.

In fact, some of the most successful cold e-mails I've ever sent started like this: "Hey man." It's casual, cool, and colloquial. I'm addressing another guy the way a good friend would, significantly bringing down the barriers between us.

If you can't distinguish the person's gender because you are contacting a company rather than a specific person, just say "Hi there."

Furthermore, starting out a message on Facebook as "Dear/Sir Madam" is ten times worse, because it implies that you are too ignorant or incompetent to customize the message based on the person's gender.

I don't mean to be harsh here, though it certainly may seem that way. Every mistake that I've laid out and picked apart in detail triggers a negative split second subconscious response in the recipient's mind, which virtually guarantees that these messages will not be returned (even if the cause is a worthy one).

**3. Make sure the message gets read.** If we send our messages to someone on Facebook and it gets filed in to their "Other" folder, then it doesn't matter if you send the most brilliant and engaging message in the history of human communication. It won't be read, and if it is, it will likely take a month or more until the recipient even sees it, a delay which invalidates most requests.

**4. Don't trigger the TLDR impulse.** TLDR is short for: "Too Long, Didn't Read." We mustn't ramble, or bunch together too many different conflicting thoughts into a small block of text. Be of singular mind and of singular purpose; thereby making the message easy to understand.

The second we start to weave together too many conflicting thoughts, mismatched metaphors, or competing threads in to one communication, the person's eyes will glaze over and we will lose their interest.

**5. Never let an e-mail be "open to interpretation."** It should be clear who we are, why we're contacting the person, and what we are interested in asking them. If our messages are too abstract or vague, it becomes infinitely more difficult for the recipient to respond.

If the sender knows nothing about the person he's contacting or the topic he's asking them about, it reflects very poorly on him. We should always do our homework, and never ask someone something that can be answered in five seconds with a Google search. By the same token, if we reach out to someone specific, we should take five seconds to search around for information about them. If we don't know anything at all about the individual whom we're contacting, what can we hope to gain from the interaction?

**6. Be mindful of the "voice" you project, and communicate on the same level as the other person.** If one were to look closely at the text in this list of mistakes, he would notice that I've consistently written "we" instead of "you," and "our" instead of "your."

Here's why: whenever addressing mistakes, weaknesses, or errors, it sounds haughty and condescending to use the "me to you" tone. It's far better for the writer to say "we" and show that he or she is not above the reader. It is simple nuances like this that make up the difference between a skilled communicator and a mediocre one - and the difference between the two can be worlds apart.

For example, take these two passages from a particular book:

*"I just want you to understand that in large part you're afraid of things that*
*are sensationalized and blown way out of proportion, and not be-*
*cause there are any real or legitimate reasons for that fear."*

Might be stronger if it read...

*"It's just important for us to understand that in large part we're*
*afraid of things that are sensationalized and blown way out of*
*proportion, and not because there are any real or legitimate reasons*
*for that fear."*

The first passage triggers resistance from the reader, by implying that the writer is above him. But the second passage, which communicates the same idea, is far more likely to evoke agreement with the reader, because the writer places herself on the same level.

The two passages are otherwise identical, but for the one tiny change, which can make an enormous difference. It's important to be mindful of the tone, or voice of your message. Which brings us to the next point...

7) **Edit out as many of the "I's," "me's," "my's," and any other pronoun that refers to yourself as possible.**

For example, instead of saying:
"I wanted to see if you could join me on my show..."

You could change it to:
"Wanted to see if you could join me on my show..."

Or even better:
"Wanted to see if you'd like to discuss your new book with my audience of listeners."

Note the ratio in each example:

Example 1) Three references to the message's sender, one to the recipient

Example 2) Two references to the sender, one to the recipient

Example 3) One reference to the sender, two to the recipient

The golden rule: within your message, it is fine to say "I," "me," and "my" a couple of times; but keep the references to the other person higher. Keep the ratio of I's, me's, and my's equal or less than the number of you's. An overuse of pronouns that reference yourself subconsciously makes the message all about you, and makes it seem that you are overly obsessed with yourself. The easy solution is to simply edit your message to remove these pronouns.

The good news is that most of these are easy to fix.

## The Art of Killer Outreach

Now that we're done focusing on horrible e-mail outreach, let's focus on the good! How's that sound? Good? Wonderful!

Here's an example of a good outreach e-mail that I received recently. It's not perfect - there is little in the way of personalization in particular - but it's certainly not half bad. Let's talk about this e-mail does right (and what could be better).

First, the e-mail starts out the right way. He e-mails my "editor" address, but correctly surmises my first name (which, as we saw in the examples above, doesn't always happen). Then he uses the first line to mention that he's been following me and praises my work. So far, so good.

Then it gets even better. Can you see what this e-mail does really well? It's there - hidden in plain sight.

What this person did exceptionally well is he engaged the so-called **"law of reciprocity."** The "law of reciprocity" is one of the six so-called "weapons of influence" detailed in the book "Influence: How and Why

People Agree to Things" by Dr. Robert Cialdini.

In his book, Cialdini describes an experiment that was performed at Cornell University in 1971 where participants of two control groups were offered to purchase a raffle ticket (the value of a ticket was twenty five cents). Group A was approached and asked directly to buy a ticket. The participants in Group B, on the other hand, were offered a Coca-Cola first.

The result? The test subjects who had received a Coke before the request was made purchased twice as many raffle tickets as the other group!

In the 1960's, the Hare Krishna religious group was in a bind financially. To solve this, they put the law of reciprocity to work. Members of the group would go to public places such as airports and approach strangers to request a donation. They quickly found out that by offering a flower to a stranger first, the recipient was much more compelled to comply with their request.

In many cases, the flower was simply disposed of after the incident. It did not matter. The flower achieved its purpose, and the religious group raised millions in funds this way. As humans, we feel compelled to return favors and help those who have helped us, even when we do so begrudgingly. Interestingly enough, the group members would visit the garbage bin, re-collect the flowers after they had been thrown out, and repeat the process.

Going back to the e-mail above, activating the obligatory nature of the law of reciprocity - where favors are returned with favors - is what this message does very well. As a fellow podcast host, he knows that reviews are important to my podcast. He offered me the proverbial „flower" to increase the likeliness that I would agree to his request.

Two other things which increased the likelihood that I would respond favorably: one, he speaks the same language as me. People in every single niche, industry, sub-group, or hobby tend to have their own "secret language" that's exclusive to them. Golfers use all kinds of slang, and so do surfers. Podcasters have their own language, and so do backpacking entrepreneurs like myself.

In his e-mail, he mentions a variety of buzzwords and topics which are near and dear to my heart: "digital nomads, getting paid to do what you love, and location independence." By dropping this language, he's showing that he's an "insider" and someone I should pay attention to.

Second (and this is something I'll touch on a bit more later), he mentions in the very beginning of the e-mail that he's following my work. If he's a subscriber to my e-mail list, or a listener to my podcast, then he falls in the group of people who allow me to do what I do. Without my audience, customers, and clients, I wouldn't be able to support myself. By being a follower of my work, increases the chances that I will respond to him favorably.

On the other hand, there is very little "What's In It For Me" factor. While I'm certainly willing to be a guest on almost anyone's podcast, even new ones with a small audience, this message features a glaring lack of a suggested benefit to me, the recipient. Further, each line begins with „We" which implies that the senders are prioritizing their own needs over my own.

## How to Write an Awesome Outreach E-mail

To score a strike in bowling, every single pin needs to be knocked down in order for it to count. Similarly, in the game of baseball, a runner needs to touch every single base in order to score a run. Even if he hits the baseball out of the park, the rules state that he must make the rounds and touch first base, second base, third, and finally home plate.

What am I getting at with this?

To perform successful e-mail outreach, there are several aspects that you need to address, or "bases" to touch in order to score a home run.

To make your e-mails most effective, there are several components that your e-mail should clearly communicate.

Your takeaway from this chapter should not simply be a breakdown of what the perfect e-mail outreach looks like from a compositional standpoint, but an understanding of the principles and nuances that make for excellent e-mail communication.

By combining these principles and nuances into one message, you can create communication (and e-mails) that become more and more irresistible.

 **John Corcoran** <johncorcoran@gmail.com>    Jan 16 ☆
to noah ▾

Hey Noah - thanks for your tweet about my Art of Manliness post mentioning you. I'm actually doing another piece for Art of Manliness about why people should share their failures, and I wanted to see if I could grab 5-7 mins of your time to talk (preferably via Skype) about your Facebook experience, and what effect talking about it openly has had on others.

The basic idea of the piece is that sharing your failures makes people more human and relatable.

Let me know if you're interested and we can set it up.

John

PS: Here's me quoting our mutual friend Andrew Warner in Forbes

PPS: Here's another Forbes piece I wrote featuring your buddy Ramit

PPPS: I love tacos too so I can't be a bad guy

# The Three C's of Your Initial E-mail

## 1. Be clear

Speak in the active tense (ie: "The dog ran into the house," not "the house was ran into by the dog"). Make sure that every word, every sentence reads clearly and there is nothing that could be misunderstood. Never put the onus on the recipient to try to translate what you're saying or what you're asking of them.

## 2. Be concise

Don't let your sentences - or paragraphs - run on for too long. Don't use more words than is necessary. Show that you respect the person's time, and that you also value your own time.

### 3. Be courteous

Provided that the person you're reaching out to is someone of repute, you should communicate with utmost respect.

My friend Sean D'Souza of "The Three Month Vacation" podcast told me his definition of a client is someone: "under your protection, care, and guidance." Likewise, Walt Disney insisted that his customers be thought of and referred to as "guests," treated just as an honored guest in one's home.

You should adopt this very mindset from the outset when you first e-mail someone. Treat the recipient of your e-mail the same way as you would an honored guest in your home. Let your words ring with politeness, respect, and courtesy.

# Compliment their work

Complimenting someone on their work is VERY effective. It is very powerful to make people feel good when they open your e-mail, because it flips a psychological switch in the recipient's brain. With your compliment, you create a positive neuro-linguistic "anchor" by associating yourself to feelings of pleasure.

When you offer your compliment, try your best to be very specific. You can mention a passage from their blog, or an article that they were featured in, and explain the effect it had on you.

A simple Google search and a bit of research can perform wonders. Check the recipient's blog, website, and social media profiles. See what they are posting and find something that you can connect over. On the flipside, few things will earn you more scorn from the outset than a lack of familiarity with the person you're attempting to connect with in the first place.

There are advanced search strings you can enter in to Google to facilitate proper due diligence before e-mailing someone. For example, recently I wanted to e-mail a reporter from National Geographic Travel about a feature I had written in Cambodia. Instead of offering some boring, abstract compliment like „I love the articles on National Geographic Travel!" I entered this specific search string into Google first:

*site:natgeotraveller.co.uk cambodia*

Here's what this does: when you enter the prefix „site:" before a search, Google will go to work to return results ONLY from the website that follows. Then you can simply add in any keywords you like after, such as „cambodia." This is a great way to find specific articles related to topics such as yours, with pinpoint accuracy.

This little technique can give us the leg up when it comes to finding something specific with which to reach out to our recipient and build rapport over. It also shows that we've done our homework.

## The Power of Positive Speech

Mark Twain said that the difference between the right word and the almost right word is the difference between lightning and a lightning bug.

This is especially true when making your first impression through e-mail outreach.

Whenever possible, I use positive subject lines (I have a full list of these with examples in my book "Buy Your Own Island").

It doesn't have to be complicated.

"Thank you!" is a great one. "Loved your article" is another. On the flipside, avoid bad, boring subject lines.

If your initial e-mail is your first impression then a great subject line is like a Berloni suit with tie. A bad or boring subject line gives off the appearance of shabbiness, unoriginality, and carelessness.

Again, it's about creating a positive psychological "anchor" so that someone perks up when they see your e-mail in the sea of messages. You want someone to welcome correspondence from you, and the easiest way to do that is by using a positive subject line.

## Subscribe to their email list

One of the easiest ways to get your foot in the door is to simply subscribe to the recipient's mailing list (or become a user of their product).

Here's why: no marketer, blogger, or entrepreneur wants to upset their e-mail subscribers - after all, subscribers comprise their primary leads and/or active clientele.

Simply becoming a subscriber of their mailing list, reader of their blog, listener of their podcast, or user of their product (whatever the case may be), increases their obligation to respond back to you in a favorable manner.

## Demonstrate Value: Occupy the Moral High Ground

*„You know, a few days ago, when we were sitting down with Barack Obama, I turned to these guys and said, ok, you know, we're making a lot of money. And yes, we're disrupting digital media. But most importantly we're making the world a better place. Through constructing elegant hierarchies for maximum code reuse and extensibility."*
*- Silicon Valley*

You should be able to demonstrate your own value and self-worth without going on for too long or rambling. One or two sentences introducing who you are and your current or past projects is enough.

Where does value come from?

Value comes from your mission - your objective. If you have a power-ful "WHY" that in and of itself is a sign of value.

Many people are like ships drifting at sea with no particular port as their destination. We never want to communicate that we are like that - aimless, without value of our own time or any worthy goal driving us.

People are drawn to others who are on an important mission, who are working on important projects.

If you don't have some "marvelous mission" that's driving your professional endeavors, then find one. It's not that hard to do: just think of the problem you solve or the benefits you provide for the people you influence. Make your mission about helping others, rather than yourself. "I want to be a millionaire" is not as compelling as "I want to create one million millionaires."

Define your ultimate mission, and that becomes your value that you can communicate to others.

# Demonstrate vulnerability

At the same time, demonstrating a chink in the armor - just a touch of vulnerability - can be very compelling. You don't want to evoke outright pity from the other person, but you don't want to be too self-assured either.

It is enough to simply show that you are human. In the book, "One Simple Idea," author Stephen Key recommends the six words: "I could use a little help," when making cold calls to gatekeepers, adding that they can be powerfully persuasive.

A simple phrase like "I could use a little help," implies that you are not perfect, that you're striving to succeed in some important endeavor, and that a small favor can help make success possible.

Also, you don't want to *inject* too much of your personality in to correspondence when first communicating with someone. Yes, you are an unique snowflake, but you don't want to project too much of that from the outset. It becomes a liability with little to no potential benefit.

It is far better to gauge the nature of the person whom you are communicating with first to see how they respond to you. Then watch how the relationship progresses to assess whether the more quirky aspects of your personality will be well-received. Being too quirky, or making jokes too early on can turn people off.

For this reason, it is far more effective to keep the tone of your initial e-mails polite, complimentary, and to the point.

## Entice and Enchant Them

I'm not a fan of offering "quid pro quo" offers to people or offering financial incentives. Few people want to be bribed, even less so by a stranger, and to come across as trying to bribe someone by appealing to their greed comes across as sleazy.

However, if you make an offer to help to promote someone else's work within your network or audience, it can go over very well.

Example:

*"John, I'm a big fan of your book, and I especially liked the part*

*about [specific details]. I'd love to help you get this message out in front of more people. I'm the host of a podcast with 20,000 monthly listeners, and would love to record an interview with you. My audience would love this. We can also add a special offer to encourage people to download your e-book."*

At the same time you entice them, you can also enchant them with a compelling story. Think about your mission (see above: Demonstrate Value) and align it to a storyline.

**Here are five examples of compelling storylines that you can adopt:**

**1. Great aspirations.** The hero wants to make the world a better place and know there must be a better way. Working nights and weekends, he creates something that people love more than their wildest dreams.

**2. David vs Goliath.** Goliath has a head start, incredible resources, and a cast of thousands. But David takes him on and defeats him, showing that the underdog can succeed.

**3. Profiles in courage.** Injustice, pain, and suffering are making our heroes' lives miserable. Despite these woes, they persevere and accomplish great things.

**4. Personal stories.** "Epic" is not always necessary. "Illustrative" is enough - talk about your personal experience doing something, or using a product.

**5. Connecting the dots.** The hero reaches a new level in her life and wants to share with others how she got there to help others who were in her situation.

If you can position what you're doing (your mission) with one of the storylines above, it can make your message much more compelling. A compelling story works especially well when contacting journalists, podcasters, and so on.

Moreover, a storyline like this can easily be adopted for your overall personal brand and message. You can adopts these storylines for uses, such as putting them on to your website, landing page, or crowdfunding page.

## Name Dropping

"Tyler said it's cool," were four words that came out of my mouth that evoked immediate and complete compliance.

What am I talking about? And who is Tyler?

Anyone who has ever tried to get access in to a hot nightclub should very well know the power of name dropping. Nightclubs are not obligated to provide access to anyone, to increase your chances of "getting in the door," it always helps if you know someone.

Here's the kicker though: as long as you know the name of an owner or manager of the club, you can in many cases "name drop" your way in the door, even if you don't actually know the person very well (or at all).

The same principle applies to any situation where you approach someone cold, whether via e-mail, a phone call, or in-person.

You can bypass a stranger's innate "I've never heard of this person" skepticism simply by associating with someone or something that they have heard of.

Let me tell you a story of a recent personal example.

During the 2012 Obama presidential campaign, I was the most successful door-to-door canvasser in Nevada, collecting the most signatures in the Las Vegas district.

Our organizers gave us a list of leads and scripts to read as we went from house to house to deliver our pitch and collect signatures. In two days of knocking on doors, I was able to collect five times more signatures than the average canvasser. By the second day, I was training the other volunteers in ways to improve their pitch.

My secret was very simple. I read over the script they handed us, and realized that were a few ways in which it could be improved upon. The key, however, was in the introduction. In the script, the introduction said something like:

*"My name is Danny, and I'm here on behalf of Organizing for America."*

I had never heard of Organizing for America, and I'm pretty sure that our prospects never had either. So instead, I made an easy and obvious change:

*"My name is Danny, and I'm here on behalf of President Obama."*

If someone knocked on your door, and told you that they had come on behalf of the president of the United States, wouldn't that arouse your curiosity?

You bet it would!

Here's the thing: all too often our messages are weak, and don't deliver an impact. You can easily make an impact in your e-mail outreach by putting the principle of association to work.

Brian Grazer, renowned Hollywood producer of "A Beautiful Mind, "Apollo 13," "The Da Vinci Code," "Arrested Development," and countless other movies and television series, used the principle of association to its utmost to build key relationships and work his way to the top of his profession.

When Brian was a very young man he got a three-month internship at Warner Brothers, where he worked as a clerk in the business affairs department, pushing a cart around.

There, he used his position to get all kinds of inside access - legal contracts, business contracts, movie proposals, and so on. He would call someone every day and say "I'm Brian Grazer. I work at Warner Brothers business affairs. I want to meet you."

He turned his three-month internship in to a year and was eventually fired, but not before selling two ideas to NBC for five thousand dollars each.

As Malcolm Gladwell, in the book "David and Goliath," elaborates: "It never occurred to the people Brian Grazer called that when he said he was Brian Grazer from Warner Brothers, what he meant was that he was Brian Grazer who pushed the mail cart around at Warner Brothers."

There are always causes, people, places, anything - that you can associate with that immediately familiarizes yourself with the recipient. By the simple act of creating this association, you are no longer a stranger, but someone who shares common interests, a kindred spirit. You can also mention a mutual friend, or connection. Or you link yourself to an authority, as Brian Grazer did at Warner Brothers and the way I did during the Las Vegas canvassing campaign.

Tim Ferriss, multiple New York Times best-selling author, and „the greatest self-promoter in the world" according to Wired magazine, has used the principle of association time and time again throughout his entrepreneurial career to catapult himself to the next level.

Before he won reknown from his books, Tim leveraged the authority and reputation of the non-profit organization in which he was a member - the Silicon Valley Association of Startup Entrepreneurs - to establish relationships with ubersuccessful entrepreneurs and mentors.

Then, years later, he leveraged the success of his first book ("The 4-Hour Workweek") to gain access to all types of people for his second and third books, "The 4-Hour Body" and "The 4-Hour Chef." He interviewed everyone from Guinness World Record holders to world-famous sous chefs to pickup artists to trainers of Olympic athletes.

Because he had already written a #1New York Times best-selling book, it was considerably easier to get all of these different types of people to agree to an interview than if he had attempted to reach out to them all prior to writing the "The 4-Hour Workweek."

Never one to miss an opportunity, Tim eventually leveraged his reputation as an author and his books to take on other industries, such as angel investing. No question about it, associating with well-known and successful brands and authority figures is one of the most powerful ways to influence others and create the types of relationships you seek.

Oh, and remember those bouncers? I would never ask for something of someone without giving something back. After they granted me access to the nightclub I would express my gratitude, and always offer to return their favor with a favor of my own: "Can I bring you a drink or something? Maybe even a water?"

If you return a gesture with a gesture it immediately resets the karmic balance. If someone grants your request, you should express your gratitude and promptly make an offer to reward their action.

As cryptic as it may sound, this also "trains" the other person neurologically to want to do things for you. It all goes back to creating an "anchor:" the action is returned with a reward, encouraging a loop of more actions and more rewards.

It sounds crazy, but it's true. I've built some of my strongest business relationships this way. I'll cold e-mailed someone else in my industry and by asking and giving back, we have been able to support one another in our respective business endeavors for years.

These business contacts are so invaluable, because of a simple bond that forms and an understanding that we will readily help one another if anything is ever needed.

## If They Don't Respond

There are a thousand reasons why someone may not respond. Influential people tend to be very busy, receive a lot of e-mail, and could miss your initial e-mail for any number of reasons (or they could simply forget to reply).

The rule of thumb is that the lack of a response usually has to do with external circumstances which are not immediately clear. It always has more to do with them than it does you, so never take it personally.

The question is: should we follow up or shrug it off and move on? And if we do follow-up, what's the best way to go about it?

Wait one week and if the person still hasn't responded, hope is not lost. In fact, it is a great opportunity to send a follow-up, and make it clear that you are awaiting some form of reply.

If one week passes, and you still have not received any reply, send a follow-up message with this subject line:

"Did you get this e-mail?"

This is perhaps my favorite subject line. It is VERY powerful.

This subject line immediately grabs their attention, and in most cases virtually compels the person to respond. You also demonstrate that you are expecting some form of reply, even if it's just to turn you down. This is important because many people slink away if they don't hear from someone and give up too easily.

Another powerful tactic you can use if you don't hear back from someone is simply to ask the person why. This encourages them to respond. There have been several instances when someone has asked something of me, and after I turn them down I wish they would ask me why. But they didn't. They simply gave up, said thanks, and went on their way with their request denied.

The principle of asking "why?" when your message is not replied to or when your request is denied is modeled after the "lost-sale close" used in sales interactions.

The lost sale close occurs after a sales interaction when a salesperson delivers his value proposition, answers the prospect's objections, and asks for the order, but the prospect still says "No," or "I'll get back to you."

Just as the salesperson is about to leave, he turns and asks:

"Mr Prospect, may I ask you a question? I've done my best to present my product in the best way I know how, but feel as though I've done something wrong. I'd appreciate it if you could you tell me something: what the real reason you didn't buy today?"

If someone doesn't respond, or says no, you can use some variant of this in your follow e-mails (just replace the interview reference to whatever you like):

"Hey Mr Smith, just a friendly follow-up :-)

If an interview is not in the cards at the moment, then that's fine, no worries.

But if possible, could you tell me the real reason why you wouldn't want me as a guest on your show? I'd like to get your feedback so I know how I can improve."

In many cases, this tactic can initiate (or reinitiate) and lead to the desirable outcome that you seek.

Oftentimes, a conversation will stale out once the other party has asked you for a proposal or asked you to present your price. You answer, and then they disappear. This happened to me recently when a company inquired about my advertising rates on my blog.

If this scenario happens to you and you don't hear back from the person after one week, send them a follow e-mail like this:

"Hi Name,

As I haven't heard back from you on this matter, I assume your priorities have changed.

Regards"

That's it. There's no secret formula, but there are ways to automate the follow-up process (see below, and next chapter for specific e-mail tools).

In a successful example of persistent follow-up in action, I reached out last year to an author to invite him to be a guest on my podcast.

First, it took several emails before he agreed, and then he suggested that it be put off until he was less busy / closer to finishing his book. The point is... this particular podcast interview was months in the making, after a good deal of back-and-forth e-mail exchanges and delays.

Nevertheless, I persistently and politely followed up at regular intervals, and continued to both offer value and demonstrate value.

Even when we first began to record the interview, I could still sense a lingering sense of apprehension and/or trepidation, until I was able to make him feel relaxed and open up.

The result?

He wrote me this follow-up e-mail to me after the interview:

*"Hi Danny,*

*It was such a pleasure speaking with you as well! Honestly, I had the best interview with you out of all the interviews I have done for the past few months. You did tons of homework and asked very insightful questions. It helped a lot to put me at ease.*

*Hope our paths will cross again in the future."*

When this guest began thinking about PR outlets for his book, he was likely thinking of established names like "Entrepreneur Magazine," "Forbes," and "INC." Chances are he had never heard of "OpenWorld" prior to my initial e-mail.

However, by observing the communication steps outlined in this chapter: by making my mission clear and by demonstrating knowledge, credibility, and value in every single interaction, I was able to win him over.

If you're an entrepreneur, even with a brand that no one has ever heard of, you can win over hearts and minds in exactly the same way. It all comes down to the way you communicate and present yourself.

## Pre-Empt a Non Response

Sometimes, I'll pre-emptively plan for a non-response and program my follow-up ahead of time. This step is especially important when I'm hired by clients to perform their outreach campaigns for them (if they don't respond, I don't get paid, so I'm highly motivated to follow up).

Let's assume that I'm contacting ten leaders within my industry with companies much larger than mine. I will immediately prepare one more message using a Streak snippet (more on Streak in chapter 4) by replying to my own e-mail thread, and then „Send Later" using the Boomerang app (more on Boomerang in chapter 3).

Using Boomerang, I will set the e-mail to send one week after my initial e-mail, and check the box „Only if nobody replies." This allows me to follow up automatically in one week if I don't receive a response from the person. Since I'm using Streak snippets, it only takes me a few seconds to prepare and send the followup.

The follow-up "snippet" that I use is typically something like this:

*„Hey Name, I just wanted to follow up on my prior email once, in case my previous email got lost in your inbox.*

*If you aren't interested, I won't take offense. If you are interested, let me know. I will send one courtesy follow-up after this email in case the timing right now does not work for you.*

*Thank you, talk soon."*

Easy, simple, and effective.

Ready to learn about more goodies and apps to increase response and automate message delivery and follow-up? Then let's proceed to the next two chapters!

# THE E-MAIL HACKER'S TOOLBOX

The applications in this chapter all integrate with Gmail, which in my opinion, is the most powerful interface because of the sheer number of free apps that can put your inbox on steroids.

## Wisestamp

**Wisestamp** is a handy-dandy that adds a fancy signature to your e-mails. It also enables you to include a photo in your signature, which adds a nice touch of personal branding. It makes your signature almost look like a business card.

The interface is super simple to set up, and takes less than five minutes. You just enter in some information in to some fields you want to include and enable it in Gmail.

Wisestamp is super-customizable, with a variety of options to customize the design of your signature. You can also include links to any number of different online profiles: Facebook, LinkedIn, Twitter, Instagram, Amazon, Google Maps, Pinterest, Flickr, and more.

There is also an option to display your latest post via Facebook, Twitter, or your blog, which is a great way to drive traffic to your site.

Wisestamp is free to use, and there is also a paid option to upgrade for even more customization features.

## Boomerang

**Boomerang** allows you to schedule e-mails to send out at a certain time. This is, hands-down, the best way to follow up with people.

Boomerang adds an extra

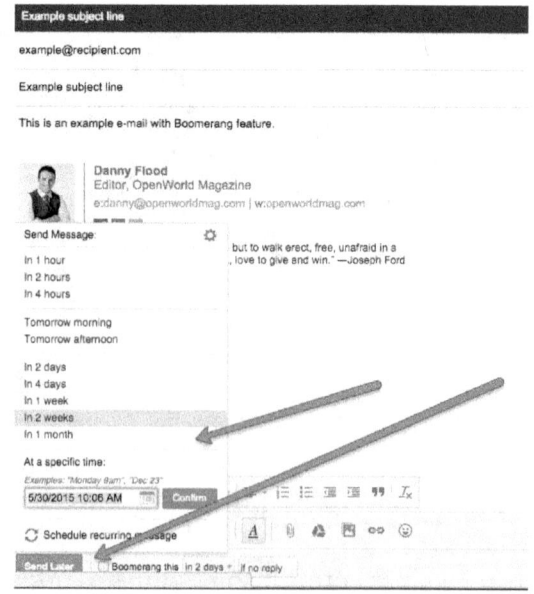

button next to your normal "Send" button at the bottom of each message with the option to "Send Later." You simply start composing an e-mail like you usually would, then hit the "Send Later" button. Another window will open promptly asking for the date which you'd like to send your message. You can choose from pre-set options: tomorrow, one week, one month, and so on, or choose a specific date on an interactive calendar.

Boomerang is ace for all of those times when someone replies back to your e-mails to say "I'm too busy at the moment, e-mail me in a month." Thanks to Boomerang, you can send back your reply immediately and make it seem like you remembered their commitment perfectly once it's finally sent. You'll never forget to follow up again. Also - remember to be VERY careful when using Boomerang. DON'T forget to click the "Send Later" button when writing your follow up. Unfortunately I speak from experience after accidentally clicking the normal "Send" button for my follow-up immediately after my initial e-mail. :(

## Batched Inbox

Every time we check our inbox, or "just check Facebook for a sec," we interrupt our train of thought, derail whatever it is we were currently doing, and get into reading and reacting mode. Reading and reacting is the opposite of proactivity, and for the purpose of peak productivity, this carries enormous implications. To drive our energy towards prolific creation and growth means taking a proactive approach to our time, and not simply reacting to new events as they occur.

How many times have you logged in to Facebook or your e-mail, becoming distracted instantly, forgetting whatever it was you wanted to accomplish in the first place? It's happened to me more times than I care to admit. Worse, for most of us, these interruptions happen several times per day - completely scrambling our priorities.

Instead of letting yourself be interrupted by new messages, you can use **Batched Inbox** to file them away in to a folder and arrive in your inbox only at certain times you set. That way you don't receive a barrage of new e-mails you have to answer every time you log in to your inbox. If you want to view your inbox normally, you can click the label "BatchedInbox."

# Inbox Pause

An alternative to Batched Inbox that I've been using for a few years is **Inbox Pause.** Inbox Pause is similar to Batched Inbox, but rather than scheduling certain times for new e-mails to be delivered, you manually "pause" and "unpause" your inbox when you are ready for new e-mails. It's a bit simpler to use, which you decide to use really depends on your personality.

If you're the more disorganized, right-brain creative type (such as me), definitely go with Inbox Pause. If you're a left-brained type, and need things to be scheduled and orderly, you will love Batched Inbox.

# Streak

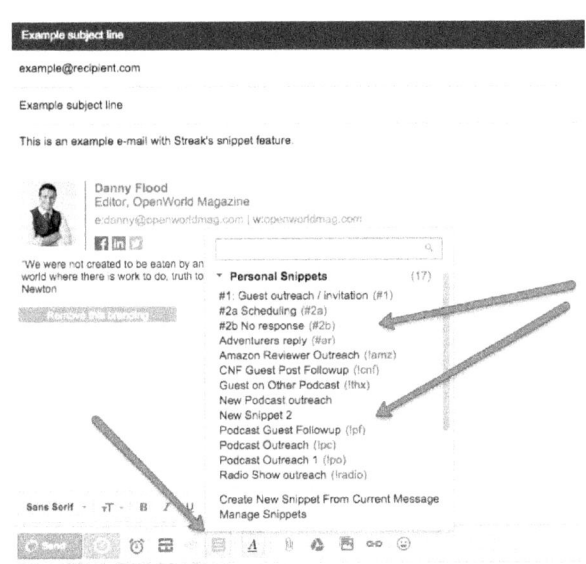

An awesome free tool, **Streak** is one of my favorite recent discoveries. One of the things that held me back from using a CRM (Client Relationship Management) service in the past was the need to learn a new interface. Streak eliminates that need by providing CRM inside of your existing Gmail account. This is a game changer and totally revamps and unlocks the power of e-mail.

Streak adds a ton of useful features to your e-mail, such as snippets, CRM pipelines, mail merges (automated customized mass e-mailing), e-mail tracking, and more. I can't think of any reason not to use it. There is a slight learning curve before you can begin using Streak effectively, so I've devoted the next chapter to sharing my favorite features that I can't live without.

## Sidekick by Hubspot

**Sidekick** has a similar feature to the e-mail tracking of Streak, but it's somewhat more powerful. Sidekick sends you real-time notifications whenever someone opens up your e-mail. You don't need to stay logged in to Gmail or even using browser for it to work; as long you are on your laptop and online, you'll receive notifications.

This is useful because it tells you the exact instant when your e-mail is opened, and most likely, responded to. Having the notifications sent to you while you work lets you follow up on their reply quickly without the need to constantly check your inbox for new messages.

Also, Sidekick also provides separate tracking for any links that you send via e-mail, including any links to your blog in your Wisestamp signature.

# Rapportive

In my opinion, you should never ever e-mail a fellow entrepreneur of even moderate influence without doing a bit of homework first.

One easy way to collect information on the fly is with **Rapportive**.

Rapportive provides real-time advanced information collection

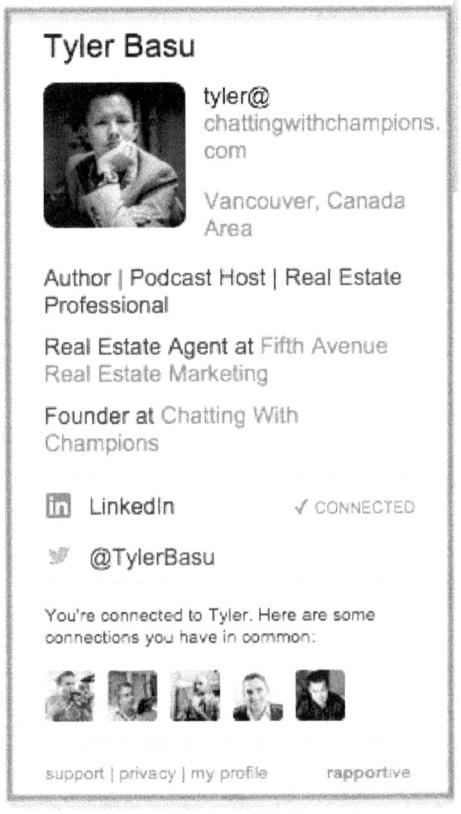

Tyler Basu

tyler@
chattingwithchampions.
com

Vancouver, Canada
Area

Author | Podcast Host | Real Estate
Professional

**Real Estate Agent at** Fifth Avenue
Real Estate Marketing

**Founder at** Chatting With
Champions

in  LinkedIn                    ✓ CONNECTED

@TylerBasu

You're connected to Tyler. Here are some
connections you have in common:

support | privacy | my profile          rapportive

in Gmail. The app creates a new window to the right of your e-mail messages with information about the sender. It will collect the title from the sender's LinkedIn profile, along with links to all of their known online properties: website, Twitter, Linkedin, and so on. The app also provides a button to directly connect with them on LinkedIn inside of Gmail.

Awesome way to personalize your e-mails on the fly, so you can build rapport, and increase response rate.

## Full Contact

**Full Contact** is like Rapportive on steroids. It collects all of the information on your contacts and aggregates all data it can find for ALL of your contacts in one place. You can browse through the Full Contact panel to find your contacts' Facebook, Instagram, Twitter, Klout Score, and more.

## Key Rocket

**Key Rocket** is helpful for learning keyboard shortcuts to compose and send e-mails quicker (for example: C button to compose a message, Tab+Enter to send).

If you're a Windows user, Key Rocket also teaches insights on how to use shortcuts to navigate other programs as well - such as Microsoft Windows, Word, Excel, Powerpoint, and so on.

## Jing

**Jing** is another free tool that has been out for a while, but it still retains its usefulness. With Jing, you can dramatically improve the communication process by recording screen-sharing videos up to five minutes in length.

How it works is simple: you click and drag the Jing icon to indicate which area of the screen you wish to record. Then after a three second countdown, the recording begins and you can start clicking, typing, or doing whatever you wish. The video also records audio, so you can begin talking as the video records your screen. This is a fantastic way to eliminate miscommunication, reduce the need for back-and-forth messaging to clarify things, and simplifies the communication process of e-mail beautifully.

Side note: There is a sister product by the same company called Camtasia, which works the exact same way as Jing but without the five minute restriction. This tool is great for creating video courses, and is the software I used to create my original WordPress Design Institute member course.

## Google Sites for Project Wikis

This is not so much a hack for the inbox, but rather something that compliments e-mail nicely.

Often, when there's an extensive deal of communication between you and a client, or between you and a contractor, a great deal of key information is exchanged over e-mail. The trouble is, when you want to go back and access the information later, it can be quite an ordeal.

For this reason, I love to use **Google Sites** to create "Project Wikis" which serve as a central repository for all information related to each project.

Google Sites is super easy to get in to. Simply Google "Google Sites" and if you're logged in to Gmail, you can create a new site with the click of a button.

You'll be given several options on the next step, click "Blank Templa-te." Trust me, it's much easier to start simple than to add dozens of features you don't need. Plus the templates on offer aren't too pretty anyhow and can be confusing to navigate. In this instance, simple is beautiful.

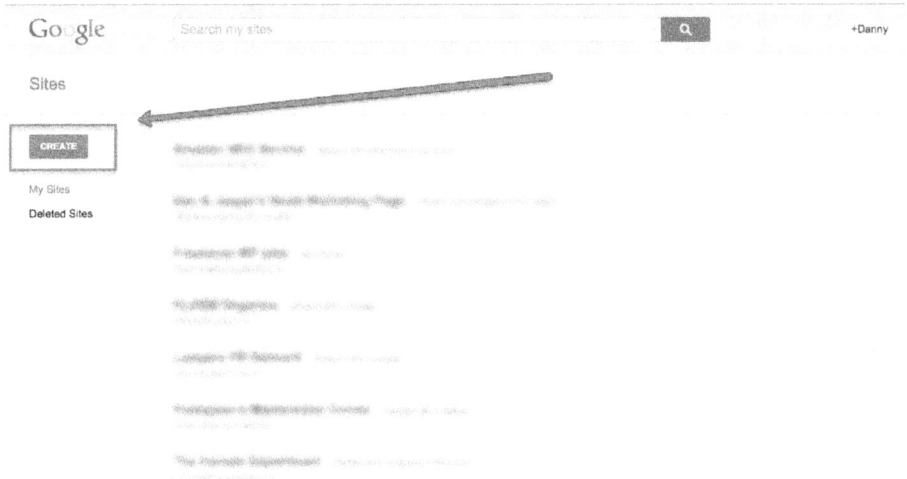

Next add a site location, fill in a captcha, and hit create. Voila, your site is now ready to go!

Adding content to your new site is as easy as a word processor. Simply add a few pages and sub-pages, and click the pencil icon for "Edit Page" and a text editor interface will pop up. In most cases, I'll simply add my notes or copy and paste important information from my e-mail.

If you click on the Gear icon for "More Options" there are a whole bunch of other things you can do with your site, but I don't recommend getting in to these until you have some experience with the user interface first. Start with the basics, and then get in to the advanced options if needed later.

Once your site is ready, you are ready to share your Google Site with your client or team members. Click "Share" and you can share a link to your new site, or invite specific people to access the site.

Google Sites are a wonderful way to organize the influx of information that you receive through e-mail, giving you one place to store logins, notes, procedures, files, and so on. Moreover, the sites sync beautifully with Google Drive, Google Sheets, and Gmail so that there's no extra hassle.

## Scheduling Apps

To be a true e-mail ninja requires the use of a good scheduling app to reduce and/or eliminate back-and-forth when it comes to scheduling appointments. Fortunately, there are a number of apps designed to suit our purpose. The process is pretty straightforward: you set up an interactive calendar with potential meeting types, list dates that you are available, along with any other information you wish to provide. You can also create fields to collect information from appointees beforehand.

Of the scheduling apps out there, which should you choose? The most popular paid option seems to be **Schedule Once** - however, this app only offers a free-trial version for 14 days. There are some free alternatives, such as **Calendly**, which offers a sleek and beautiful calendar design. Unfortunately the free version of Calendly only allows one event type.

The scheduling app that I'm currently using is **Acuity Scheduling**. It is free, it allows me to create multiple types of events and appointments, and is extremely to set up and use: a trifecta. Once my calendar is set up with all of my desired appointments, I simply need to copy and paste a link to my schedule and the recipient will be lead to my Acuity calendar to schedule an appointment and fill out any requests for information.

I use my scheduling app mainly for consultations and podcast interviews, and it dramatically simplifies the ease of scheduling appointments with my clients and interviewees.

## Taming the Beast

This last set of suggestions for increasing e-mail productivity have nothing to with apps at all - they are simply small suggestions which can make a big difference in taming your e-mail and other message inboxes and feeds so that they don't run your life.

Sometimes the key to productivity is not about adding anything at all. Sometimes it's about resolving to do without.

There are several time-wasting activities that I've eliminated or dramatically minimized to control the influx of information and protect my productivity:

**1. Facebook newsfeed.** Facebook's user base is larger than the population of China, so one can only imagine how many billions of hours are lost to browsing the newsfeed. Never mind Farmville or Bejewelled. The newsfeed is a rabbit hole that will steal your focus like a thief in the night.

Here's what to do instead: Instead of logging into Facebook at face-book.com (the default), start logging in to the URL: facebook.com/messages instead. This allows you to tame Facebook once and for all by bypassing the newsfeed, and log in directly to your inbox :-) Enormous productivity-saver.

**2. Twitter newsfeed.** You can bypass other newsfeeds, such as Twitter, in much the same way. When I need to check my Twitter I log in to my profile URL directly (twitter.com/dandanflood) instead of Twitter.com, so that I don't allow myself to get distracted by recent items.

**3. Working without wifi.** One of the best ways to get through e-mail faster is to simply write your e-mails in a Word document, and then send them once you are online. It is amazing how much quicker I am able to write the day's e-mails this way, without having to sort and sift through my inbox, write an e-mail, sort and sift again, and write yet again.

No fancy tech needed, you simply create a list of all the people you need to e-mail for the day, and begin writing your e-mails. There is also an app called "Gmail Offline" which allows you to read and write e-mails without an internet connection, but I much prefer simply writing in to a document.

# CRM FOR GMAIL - STREAMLINE THE PROCESS

One of the most powerful ways to take your lead generation to the next level is with CRM software. Enter Streak. A free add-on for Gmail that will turn you into an e-mail marketer overnight.

## Intro

"CRM" which stands for "client relationship management" can be a confusing thing to learn for anyone who lacks training as a corporate sales professional. Moreover, the array of complex SAAS (another fancypants acronym which stands for "software as a service) CRM tools out there are bulky and difficult to learn or use. Further exacerbating the problem is the lack of layman's tutorials which make the process of learning how to use CRM software effectively.

For me personally, CRM was always one of those things that I felt I "should do," but could never work up the justification to actually try. It seemed like the stuff of sales professionals at large organizations - not for entrepreneurs.

Then I found out about Streak, the free CRM app for Gmail, from my friend Nick Loper - and it changed everything.

There is a bit of a learning curve before you can begin to use Streak to its full potential. However, once you do, it multiplies your capabilities to use e-mail effectively. It can save hours of time spent using e-mailing each week, and free up your time to do other things. It amplifies your ability to promote yourself and your business, making it super simple to generate leads new leads as well as follow up with past connections and clientele.

Point blank: you need CRM if you're serious about growing your business, one relationship at a time, and Streak is the easiest free solution I've found. In this chapter, I'll start out by introducing you to some of

the most practical features of Streak that you can begin using immediately to improve your e-mail hacking skills.

# Snippets

One of the most
useful features is
the ability to create
"snippets." Snippets
are pre-made tem-
plates for messages
that you send often.

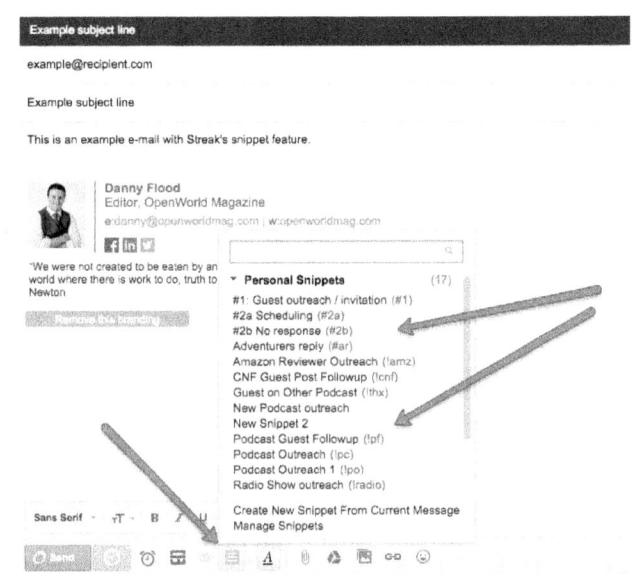

You simply create them once and then create a "shortcut" snippet that
automatically reloads the template. This saves a TON of time and is
great for follow-up or pitching. It's far superior to the old school copy
and paste in a number of ways.

1. No need to copy and paste both the title of the e-mail and the body

2. No need to write or search for the original source to copy and paste
- Streak stores it inside of Gmail

3. Copy and paste only allows one thing to be copied and pasted at a
time. Streak stores as many snippets as you want, and you can insert

them into e-mail instantly.

To begin using snippets is easy. Simply begin composing a message, then click on the orange Streak icon at the bottom of the e-mail composer. You can then select "Create a New Snippet from E-mail" or "Manage Snippets."

You then simply adjust your template, an edit the body or title of the e-mail. Then you can assign a name to the snippet, and some shortcut text. For example, your shortcut might be: !followup - or a set of initials. I always start my snippets with an ! mark so that they don't get inserted by accident when I'm typing an e-mail.

That's it. Once your snippet is saved, it's available to you forever. Simply enter the shortcut text and you can re-use the snippets for e-mails that you send over and over again.

## Track Whether Your E-Mails Have Been Opened

Streak has several other unique features for you to play around with. One feature is automatic: it adds an eyeball icon next to your sent messages to let you know whether the e-mail has been viewed by the

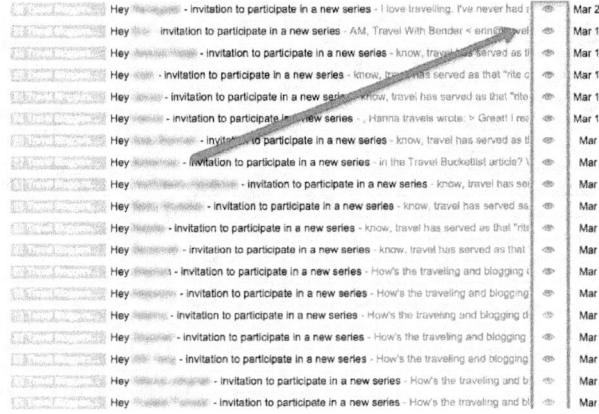

recipient or not. This is known as "e-mail tracking."

A grey eyeball indicates that the e-mail has not been opened, while a green one reveals that it has been. An invaluable feature that tells you whether your e-mails are being read or not, facilitating the proper follow-up strategy.

## Pipelines

Another feature that implements nicely with Streak's other abilities is called "Pipelines."

Pipelines allow you to organize groups of leads by category and save important information which will be instrumental for your outreach campaigns. These categories also neatly organize your e-mails into corresponding "Boxes" within your inbox.

Start by adding, subtracting, and organizing the custom fields where you plan to input information about your contacts.

Click on the small arrow next to a column title and you will have the option to insert new columns. Choose "Free Form" and you can create any type of custom field you like - some good ones might be Website, Business Name, Email, and so on.

If you click the "More" tab, you will be given the option to import contact information via a CSV. For this feature, I highly recommend you use Google Sheets. To make the import work, the titles of the columns you use in your CSV (spreadsheet) need to match and align perfectly with the titles of the columns in your Streak pipeline.

For instance, if your Streak Pipeline uses the following column titles:

"Name | Email | Website | Business"

Then your spreadsheet needs to have the following column titles as well:

"Name | Email | Website | Business"

If the titles of the columns don't match, then the attempt to import your contacts will fail.

Pipelines provide increasing returns with the more leads you have, and the larger your team is. If you only have 5 or 6 leads, than it may not be worth it to create pipelines.

However, if you mass import data using spreadsheets and integrate your pipelines with the Mail Merge feature described in the next couple of pages, it can prove to be extremely effective.

## Google Sheets

When entering mass data into your pipelines from spreadsheets, the option that works most seamlessly are Google Sheets. For one reason or another, external programs do not import into Streak as well and when I first began trying to import my data I kept running in to issues which would prevent the operation from completing.

From what I found the cause of the issues usually has to do with certain meta-data or unique character types. For example, different text editors may use a different version of a comma, or an apostrophe. One might require a straight apostrophe, while a "rich text editor" may create curved apostrophes. Minor things like this can cause an import to fail.

Fortunately, Google Sheets is a free cloud-based option, and it is easy to transfer data from external sources. If you use software like Microsoft Excel or iWork Numbers, export your spreadsheet to a CSV and then copy all of the fields you wish within your CSV and paste them into Google Sheets.

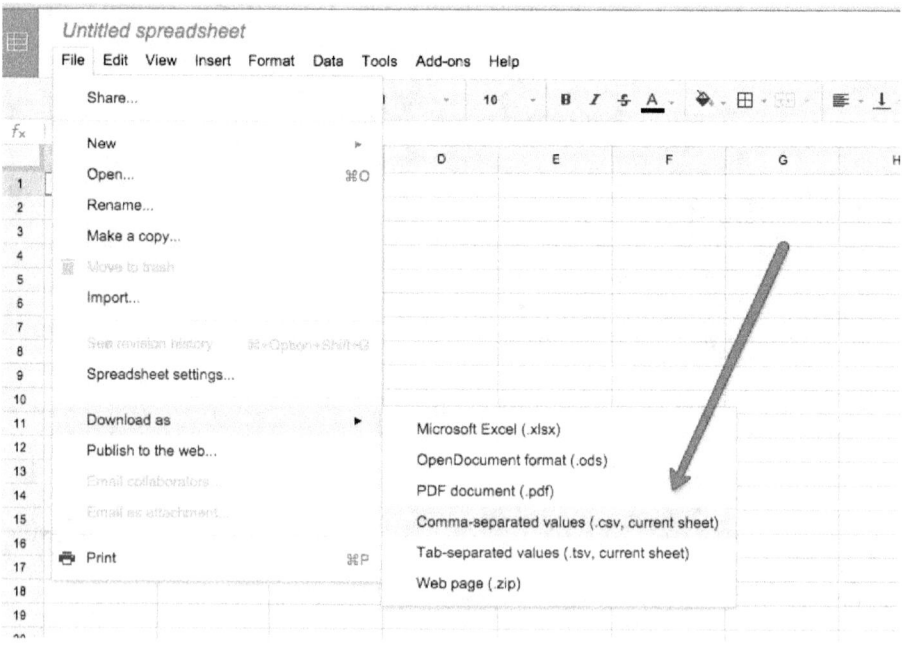

Once your spreadsheet is ready to go in Google Sheets, it is very easy to input the information in to Streak. Simply choose "File," then "Download as Comma-separated Values" then you'll be ready to import your data into a new pipeline inside Streak!

## Mail Merge

Mail Merge? What does mail merge mean exactly?

...That was my reaction when I first heard about this feature. Here's what it really means: mass customized e-mails. In other words, it's the equivalent of the ultimate shadow ninja mass duplication technique.

Imagine a team of ninjas, all carbon copies of you, sending out your e-mails customized to each recipient, one by one.

It's pretty cool.

Mail merge is pretty straightforward to use, and if your pipeline is set up correctly then you can begin to use this very effective and useful feature in just a few steps.

Start by composing a new e-mail and clicking the "Mail Merge" link to the top right of your message. Write the e-mail you would like to send (or better yet, use a snippet), and choose your Pipeline. You can then check the boxes for which recipients you would like to target with the Mail Merge (note that you are only able to send batches of 50 per mail merge, and Gmail has its own daily send limit of 500 messages per day).

With this done, the only step left is to insert custom fields to match up with fields that are in the pipeline you plan to use. See the notice at the bottom that says "Want to customize each email (e.g greeting)?" Click the blue "Insert Template" link and select a custom field such as "Name," "Business," or "Website."

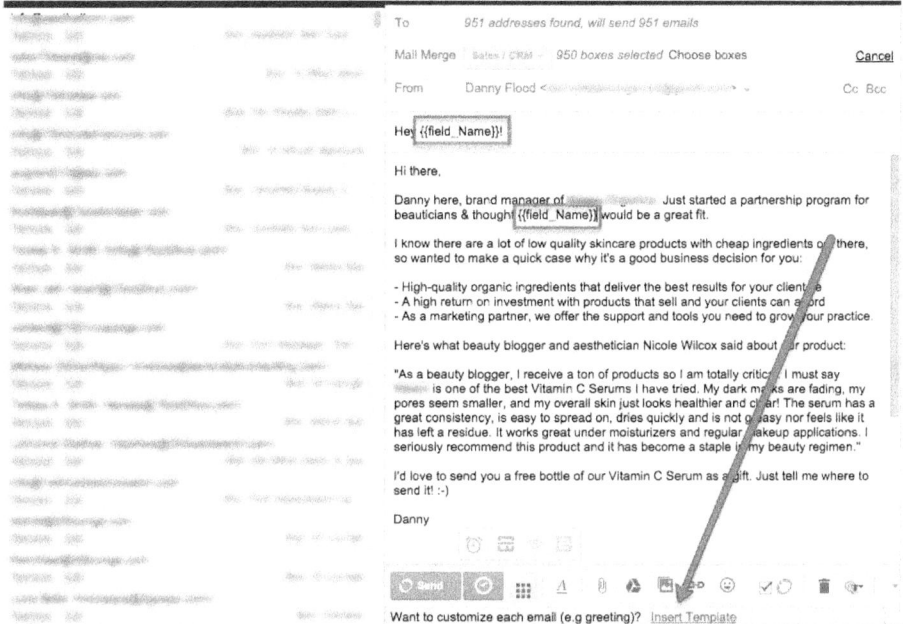

As you can see in this example, {{field_Name}} in this message becomes customized to reflect the data you enter in the {{field_Name}} category of your pipeline. You can customize your message to input any custom data you choose, for example if you add a field for "Website" or "Business," then Mail Merge will pull the data from your pipeline and insert each individual field customized for each individual.

Mail Merge will then begin e-mailing everyone that you select within your pipeline, one by one. Needless to say, this feature is VERY powerful - a huge way to use technology to gain greater leverage for your time.

Streak has a variety of different features to choose from beyond the ones listed here, but these are the ones I use the most.

In the next chapter, we'll explore several techniques to find leads to contact, so that you can begin to put these strategies into action!

# HOW TO GROW YOUR NETWORK AND FIND PEOPLE TO CONTACT

Now that our approach to e-mail outreach is grounded in good, solid communication and we have the tools needed to be successful, let's explore some strategies to find the people we want to connect with!

While I confess to be a bit of a technocrat who spends far too much time online, none of these solutions are extraordinarily complex or require advanced technical knowledge. You don't need any programming experience or need to know how to use web scraping tools. I prefer to draw upon powerful features and strategies using many of the tools that we already use, features that few of us actually know about.

The good news is that anyone - from beginner to expert - can use these techniques, and in many cases I've provided example strings that you can simply copy and paste into a database.

With that intro aside, let's discuss the one caveat...

## The Magic Bullet?

If you're hoping to find a magic bullet that automates the lead harvesting process with no effort on your part, then skip to the next chapter.

I wish that I could present some unbeatable, automated way to harvest the leads you want with the least amount of effort. I've done a ton of research to try to find some secret solution that few know about. Unfortunately I haven't found it.

There is no "secret formula" really when it comes to generating leads, at least from what I've found. However, there are different means suited to different purposes - which we'll cover in this chapter - and there is one best way which you may or may not expect!

If there is any semi-automated way to get high quality contacts with minimal effort, it's through warm referrals. I have so many connections made on my behalf these days that I don't necessarily need to perform cold outreach unless I choose to.

I realize that not everyone starts here, however if you follow some of the best practices in this book to build up a network base, you'll soon find more and more of the connections you want coming away with less direct effort on your part.

Simple right? If you take the time to build some really good quality connections and keep giving those people value, you'll find that doors will continue to open for you.

You can use some of the web apps mentioned in this book such as Streak and Boomerang to make your e-mail practices and follow ups more orderly and efficient. If you make it a priority to stay in touch and keep these relationships strong, they will blossom and the effort you put forth will come back to you.

**The formula is simple: always be giving value.** When you follow up, always adopt a mindset of value-giving instead of value-taking.

For example, recently I reached out cold to an editor for Yahoo! Travel. Her response was quite favorable, as she responded very positively to my work. She sent over a list of requirements to participate as a contributor. I responded thanking her for her positive reply, enthusiastically filling out everything she had asked me for, and then... silence.

I could have pressed the issue by asking "Did you get this e-mail?" and forcing a reply, but as she had already replied back favorably I didn't feel a need to present a challenge in this case.

Instead, I followed up cordially to check in and tell her about an incredible traveler whom I had just interviewed on my podcast. The interview was extremely successful, drawing tens of thousands of listens, and it could make a great story for her publication as well.

Might she be interested in an introduction?

Then at the bottom of my e-mail, very casually, I included a PS (post-script) and asked, "By the way..." to check in on the item we had discussed before.

This is a textbook example of adopting a mindset of giving value with your approach. Any time we create value for others, we indirectly create value for ourselves and keep our relationships strong.

It's strong relationships that open doors and facilitate an endless chain of referrals, and the moral compass of humanity dictates that favors are returned with favors.

## How to 10x Reach of Your Network with Minimal Effort

In his book, "Never Eat Alone," Keith Ferrazzi points out that the true power of networks lies in acquaintances, distant acquaintances, and friends of friends.

One of the easiest and most powerful ways that I've found to multiply my circle of influence with very little effort is to create a mastermind group and invite the top professionals within my niche to join. The group meets once monthly through Google Hangout, and we help each other by sharing advice, resources, and connections.

As it turns out, when I created a mastermind for podcasters, two of the other members already had their own lists of contacts of other podcasters that they had created to promote their own products and projects. We created a Google Sheet where so that we could share helpful contacts. Since Google Sheets is entirely in the cloud, it can be shared and edited by anyone you wish.

Within a couple of weeks, we had compiled our contacts together and had an excel sheet of nearly 300 contacts in this niche, with first and last names, e-mail, website, and the name of their brand. Plus, we shared mutual connections in common with everyone on the list that we could play up and use to set up introductions.

Very powerful stuff.

When it comes to inviting members to your mastermind, aim as high as your reach will let you. I always shoot for 5-6 active members in any mastermind group that I put together. Too few members, and the group falls short of the critical mass needed to get a discussion going, and too many members dilutes the focus and attention that each member receives.

By the way - I've plugged Google Sheets elsewhere in this book; and also recommend Sheets for organizing contacts within different niches, along with their website, blog, and contact information (you'll also remember that Sheets integrates seamlessly with Streak).

For example, if you're an author you may create a list of journalists, podcast hosts, and PR outlets. If you're an actor, you could create a list of talent agents and producers.

## Search Tools and Tricks

Perhaps the most powerful tools to find people involve basic search engines. I'm talking about Google, Facebook, and LinkedIn. Each has its own capabilities and caveats, some of which are better suited and more powerful for certain purposes.

## Google

With Google you have...

1. The world's most powerful search engine
2. Advanced search strings to pinpoint information
3. Image search

**Why It Rocks:**

These days you can Google almost anyone and find a way to contact them. There's virtually no business executive, entrepreneur, CEO, journalist, blogger, podcaster, that can't be found through a simple Google Search of their name.

**Advanced Google Search Strings**

These are some advanced search strings which I find helpful for finding either specific people to contact or to find specific data on individual persons before I contact them.

Two very simple ones which I use often are:

Search by site: site:domain.com
Search a niche: related:domain.com

You can also search someone by name and exclude their own domain from the search. This is a useful way to find external pages where the person is featured. Great way to see who they interact with, what PR outlets have covered them, and so on.

Simply add an "-" in front of the domain which you would like to exclude.

Example: danny flood -openworldmag.com -danny-flood.com -lavalinkonline.com
(openworldmag.com, danny-flood.com, and lavalinkonline.com are all domains that I own)

Other useful options are to search using @ (for social tags) or with a hashtag. Examples:

*@dandanflood*
*#digitalnomad*

**Image Search**

One of the most interesting and unique ways to use Google is to use their lesser-traffic Image Search function (images.google.com).

With Image Search, you can search the normal way using keywords, but you can also click and drag any image in to the search bar.

For example, you can find blogs that have covered products similar to yours by adding an image of the product. This is a great way to get coverage for your own products. An obvious application might be for crowdfunding. You could easily find bloggers or journalists who have supported crowdfunding projects similar to yours.

Image Search is a wonderfully effective way to see what your competitors are up to. You can search for any brand and see who is covering them (and gain a clear picture of their marketing channels at the same time). If you hover over any image result, it will reveal the domain where the image appears.

This is a great way to find guest blogging opportunities. You can search a competitor in your niche, then save each domain, article writer, and webpage URL to a document.

To confirm an e-mail address for an individual, there are a number of options you can try, such as Mailtester (mailtester.com), or emailgenerator.io.

Since I'm a fan of gaining leverage whenever possible, my favorite tool for confirming e-mail addresses is **Toofr**. Toofr works the same as emailgenerator.io, but it eliminates the unnecessary step of validating potential e-mail addresses manually.

Toofr is very simple to use: enter in the first and last name of the person, their domain, and Toofr will search multiple properties and profiles on a variety of sites (such as Facebook, Twitter, Foursquare, Klout, WordPress, about.me, and so on) to confirm their e-mail address.

You can sign up for a free Toofr account and get 50 "credits" to test out the service. In most cases, a quick name and domain search won't even use up one credit. There are also paid options with even more features.

A quick search on Toofr (or even Google) will reveal the contact for the writer of each article so you can request your own interview. Then all you have to do is compose a new message in Gmail, and enter the e-mail address that Toofr provides. If it's a valid address, you should see a social media profile listed on the right hand side of your browser - either from Google+ or LinkedIn via Rapportive (make sure that you are composing the e-mail in the fly-out window, and not in full screen, or it will not work - see below).

If you have a list of contacts with a first and last name, and a domain, you can use Toofr and within 10-15 minutes you can harvest the contact information for ten people and send out ten different e-mails.

You already have a talking point in place to pivot from to build instant rapport: "Loved your interview on [Competitor XYZ], (and I'd love to contribute value in my own way, here's how...)"

Don't forget to use Streak snippets.

Also, Google Image Search is one of the most effective ways to find websites (especially blogs) around a certain topic that you would not find through a normal web search.

For example, when researching for an article a very small town in Mexico that I visited during a trip, I chanced upon the blog of Tony Mangan, who ran through that very same town during his "world run." Tony and I connected afterwards, and have been friends since. But I never would have found him if not for Google's Image Search.

# Facebook

With Facebook you have...

Graph search

Mutual friends

Friend suggestion feature

Facebook Groups for virtually any interest or niche

**Why It Rocks:**

Facebook is, hands down, the most personal way to interact online (if online interactions can be considered personal).

Moreover, Facebook's search is actually quite useful, in more ways than one. One of the best ways to use Facebook to find the people you want to connect with is using Facebook Graph Search.

For instance, you can type the following in to Facebook's search bar:

*friends of friends who live in [location]*

And Facebook will give you a long list of second degree connections that you have in that location, and show you what mutual friends you have in common. You can also refine the search to:

*friends of [specific person] who live in [location]*

There are a number of different search strings you can use in Facebook, for example you can search by interests as well:

*People who like cycling in Austin, Texas*

For more information on these search strings I direct you to Facebook's site: **www.facebook.com/about/graphsearch**)

**Facebook Groups**

Facebook groups, on the other hand, are a powerful way to leverage your time. You simply write one message, post it within a group, and the leads come to you!

There are thousands of Facebook Groups out there devoted to every type of niche, industry, and interest you can imagine. To make it work, however, you really need to personify the principle of giving value versus taking value. Self-promotion is always value-taking because you're attempting to take from the group to benefit yourself, and falls flat.

Instead, offer something to the group without immediately asking for anything in return. In doing so, you will often discover prospects who will be interested in working with you in one way or another in the near future.

Value-giving can come in the form of valuable advice (if you're an expert in a certain area), or it can come in the form of a free sample. To make it work, align yourself to a niche where you can provide a certain benefit. For example, authors want more publicity for them-selves and more sales for their books. Bloggers want more publicity for themselves, and they want their blogs to load faster. Golfers want to add 10 yards to their drives while simultaneously curing their slice.

There are Facebook groups of hungry people in each of these niches, and plenty more, actively seeking out both benefits and solutions to their problems - both of which you can offer to them.

Opportunities to generate business through Facebook Groups are everywhere, if you can 1) provide a benefit that these people want, 2) present it in a way that gives them value, and 3) do so without promoting yourself.

## Facebook Groups for Geographic Locations

Facebook Groups are also my favorite way to network when I travel. Before making a trip to a new destination, I'll search the city and see what kind of groups exist. Expat groups, locals groups, and Couch-Surfing groups exist for virtually every city on the planet.

A few days before my arrival date, I'll post in each of these groups to introduce myself, say a few cool things about me (these days I usually demonstrate value by providing a link to my Amazon author page - everyone loves to meet an author!), and mention that I'm coming on a certain date and would love to meet up. I've made a bunch of great connections this way, including many strong business contacts. Consult the section called "Demonstrate Value" in chapter 2 for ideas on what to write.

Again, Facebook Groups are a great way to leverage your time because instead of sending messages one-to-one, you can post one message and potentially reach thousands. The amount of effort is the same.

# LinkedIn

**With LinkedIn you have...**

Advanced search tools like RecruitEm
In-Mails with LinkedIn's Sales Premium Account

**Why It Rocks:**

LinkedIn is the leading social media platform for business executives. There's a lot of connections and deals to be made if you know how to find and connect with the right people for your business on LinkedIn.

I go in to quite a bit of detail on how to use RecruitEm and LinkedIn's Sales Premium option in tandem to build relationships with influencers on LinkedIn and land jobs and contracts in my book, **"Buy Your Own Island."**

To summarize, there is an excellent free tool used by recruiters called

"RecruitEm" (recruitin.net) which uses precise search strings on Google search to pinpoint the people you want to find on LinkedIn, Google+, Stack Overflow, and GitHub. You simply enter a few fields as criteria, and can extract results by country, job title, and other relevant keywords.

Once you find the right person to contact, the best way to reach them is with a LinkedIn Sales Premium account. A paid account allows you to cut through much of the clutter by sending In-Mails, and LinkedIn will "replenish" your In-Mail credits whenever you don't receive a reply from someone.

There are a number of other great ways to use LinkedIn to find people to connect with; though I personally don't use LinkedIn all that much, as it's targeted more to corporate professionals than to entrepreneurs.

Life-Long Learner has some great tips for using LinkedIn, so if interested **check out this free podcast episode here** (fast forward to 7:50 for LinkedIn strategies).

# Twitter

## With Twitter you have...

Hashtag / Handle search

View user interactions and other information

Automated features

Open-source API

## Why it Rocks:

Twitter seems to have less restrictions than other social media platforms like Facebook and LinkedIn, which means you can do a lot more with it. The possibilities for developers to create tools (see Triberr in the next section) that provide unique features seem to be endless with Twitter's API.

For example, one thing I love about Twitter is the ability to send automated messages to new followers. You can set up automated direct messages for free this using the app **Crowdfire.** That said, an awful lot of people are also sending out automated messages, so if you set this up it's important to be a little bit different.

From what I've seen, most people will send some form of automated message that says something like "Thanks for the follow! How are you?" or "Follow me on Facebook too!" or "Check out my blog: (link)."

All of this stuff is just pushing of clutter, though. If there's no incentive for them to do as you ask, then what's the use? If you do send out automated messages, I highly recommend to create a landing page and then offer followers something for free (I send them to a page with an offer to download my free audiobook).

That way, you'll dramatically increase the conversion rates of your automated direct messages and gain new subscribers for your e-mail list.

In terms of outreach, Twitter is perhaps the best way to get on to someone's radar quickly. You can easily follow a number of influential people at the same time, and begin interacting with them immediately in a low-pressure way, such as re-tweeting their shares, an excellent way to warm the relationship before you contact them.

It's also very easy to discover a individual person's Twitter profile, as Twitter performs very well in Google Search. Searching by hashtag (e.g. #digitalnomad) is a great way to discover what's going on in a particular niche, find people to connect with, and get on their radar by re-tweeting their content.

Twitter's own native search engine isn't very useful; fortunately there are a number of external programs for Twitter which are. One of my favorites that I've been using a lot lately is **Twtrland**.

Twtrland pulls up all kinds of advanced data from Twitter, and one of the easiest ways to use it to research people is to go to:

*twtrland.com/profile/twitterhandle*

Example:

*twtrland.com/profile/dandanflood* (my personal Twitter handle)

This URL will provide a bunch of advanced data about the user, such as the content they post, how often they post, their demographics, and their responsiveness. Also, if you add /conversations to the end of the URL above, it will show you who they interact the most with!

Example:

*http://twtrland.com/profile/dandanflood/conversations*

This is a great way to find out who their friends and acquaintances are, both personally and professionally.

Twtrland has several other features to play around with, but these are the ones I find the most useful. It's always helpful when you research someone to see how they interact with, and two of my favorite ways to do this are with Twtrland and the exclusion search string listed in the Google section above.

## Build Your Tribe

If you're blogging (and you should be), then I highly recommend Triberr (triberr.com), one of my favorite ways to increase both the leverage of my blog and social media platforms.

What is it?

Triberr is a platform that integrates seamlessly with your blog and shares your new posts to a "tribal stream," where other members of your tribe can easily and automatically share your posts on their Twitter accounts. They can also read your articles in Triberr, and comment.

Besides the immediate benefit of sharing content with your "tribe," Triberr is a wonderful way to both find influential people and build influence at the same time.

Active Triberr users have a "help each other out" mentality by default; and Triberr communities are a fantastic way to build relationships with top influencers in your niche over time. It also allows you to 10x your reach across social media (I'm currently in seven tribes with a reach of over 1.5 million), automate your Twitter updates with relevant content, and it's free!

What's not to love?

To make Triberr work for you, you need to start your own tribe. Then search for other tribes within your niche, and begin inviting members. Triberr shows you the reach each person has on their profile, and the power of your tribe really comes when you combine your collective reach, so numbers matter.

As you grow your own tribe, ask to be invited to other tribes. You can message a chief directly, invite them to your tribe, and ask to be added to theres.

For more on how to ace Triberr and its many benefits, I refer you to this article from my friend Ryan Biddulph (whom I incidentally connected with through Triberr).

The point is that Triberr is a platform which allows you to easily connect with top influencers in a niche, interact with them, and share their content. When you share their content on your Twitter feed, they take notice, and your name will register in their mind more and more. Plus, the reciprocity aspect is already built in to the procedure. This is a very effective way to nurture the types of relationships you want prior to performing e-mail outreach.

By the way, Twitter is a useful platform to focus on if you want to improve your prospects for e-mail outreach. This is because many view the size of your Twitter following as an indicator of perceived influence and importance. Many PR companies, for instance, will not even consider working with a client with under 10,000 Twitter followers. A large Twitter following will also make it easier to receive invitations to other tribes on Triberr.

The fact of that matter is, numbers matter.

How you choose to gain this following is up to you - there are a variety of black hat, white hat, and grey hat methods for acquiring followers in social media. There are several useful articles on Medium.com which will teach you how to build up your follower base, simply type this in to Google: "site:medium.com grow twitter followers" and peruse.

I will say this: I'm a big fan of automation through technology, so long as it's done in an ethical manner which doesn't harm or spam anyone.

I confess that I never placed much stock in Twitter until discovering Triberr, always believing that social media management was too time-intensive for the reward it provided. Triberr allows you to have your cake and eat it too - highly recommend to check it out and learn how it works.

# In Summary

There are, no doubt, a hundred other ways to build your network, warm relationships, and find people you wish to contact. Perhaps a thousand. Rather than provide a trite reference of all the different options, I listed these because they are some of the best ways that are working for me right now. All of the tools and techniques in this chapter - such as Toofr, RecruitEm, Triberr, Twtrland, Google exclusion search, and so on - provide a tremendous amount of leverage.

My aim is to help you be as effective as you can be given the time and resources you currently have at your disposal. If you have a suggestion that I should include in this chapter, please let me know.

Write in to me at: danny@openworldmag.com with the subject line "E-mail hacking book" and let me know your thoughts.

Keep reading for an excellent e-mail outreach case study by Nick Loper in the next chapter, followed by some closing words from me, and a list of all resources mentioned in this book.

# ADHERENCE: MAKING THE
# OUTREACH HABIT STICK

"Acquaintances, in short, represent a source of social power, and the
more acquaintances you have, the more powerful you are."
-Malcolm Gladwell

In the book, "Never Eat Alone" author Keith Ferrazzi shares the account of his CEO friend who attributes his success to "talking to fifty people every day."

After reading Mr Ferrazzi's book I tried this. I contacted a bunch of people I barely knew and probably had no business reaching out to in the first place. My goal was to get as close to the target of fifty people as I could.

It went nowhere.

Talking to fifty people every day might be fine if we were the CEO of a huge company with hundreds of employees, but for the rest of us its a bit excessive. Shotgun networking burns us out faster than Melisandre from "Game of Thrones" burns her human sacrifices - and it doesn't work.

If we set a goal to talk to fifty people seven days a week it would be impossible to have anything more than a shallow, surface-level interaction. We would spread ourselves too thin. It would exacerbate the difficulty to follow up and realize anything productive from these interactions.

Overwhelming ourselves sets us up for failure. There is a point when too much becomes too much. To make good on the strategies in this book, I recommend adhering to a simple, but diligent approach that is easy to stick with.

We want to set a schedule with a minimal and easy to meet requirement so that we can practice e-mail outreach and turn it into a consistent habit.

We have an extensive collection of techniques and tools at our disposal, but nothing in this book will make any difference unless we integrate these into our workflow, practice, and keep consistent!

## Three Times a Week for 30 Days

There's a saying that we need to practice something for at least 30 days before it becomes a habit. Our goal should be to commit to a consistent schedule to develop the habit of e-mail outreach and improve over time.

You'll also find that this habit leads to more opportunities coming your way - and more money. It's the result of being persistent, getting in front of people, and constantly following up. Most people do not follow-up, they slink away with tails tucked between the legs.

So, here's what I do.

I make it a habit to proactively reach out to (or follow up with) ten new people every Monday, Wednesday, and Friday. I do it first thing in the morning, after breakfast, a workout, and a short meditation. I try to power through these e-mails in an hour or two, and respond to any items that need my attention.

The composition of your outreach e-mail doesn't need to be complicated. Make it really simple so that the consistency habit develops and - most importantly - sticks.

For example, if you have contacts or clients you haven't talked to in a while, just send them something like:

"Hey [Name] - it's been a while and just wanted to check in. How's your business doing? What have you been up to? Would love to catch up when you have time."

A simple message like this can re-initiate the dialogue between you and a client you've worked with in the past. It creates opportunities to work with them again, or generate referrals. Bringing past clientele back from the brink is a more efficient way to create business than advertising for new clients.

*Reach out - Close the Deal*

The other classic scenario is the prospective lead who inquires to ask you about your services: whether it's a consultation / rates card / proposal, then disappears after you respond.

Raise your hand if you've ever found yourself in this situation. It's happened to me more times than I can count.

Here's what you do. Simply send something like this:

*"Hi [Name] - as I haven't heard back from you on this, I assume your priorities have changed."*

Copy and paste these examples if you like; the key is to just get into the habit of proactively reaching out to ten people every Monday, Wednesday, and Friday.

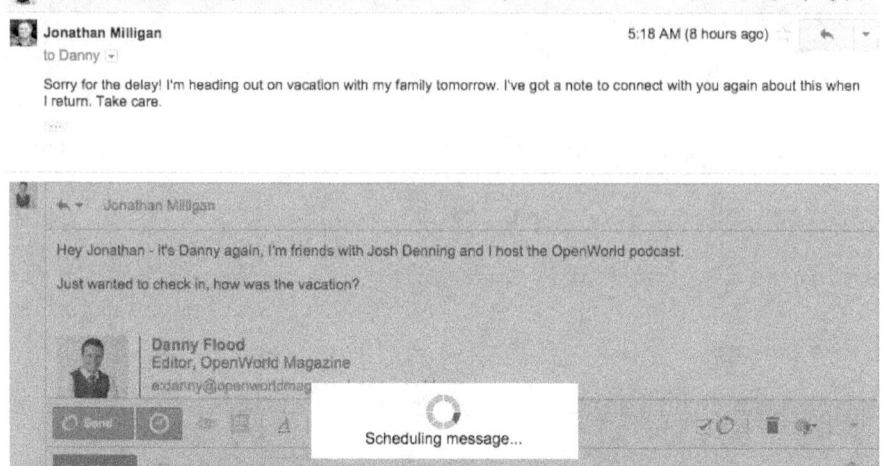

# An Example Workflow

I keep a notebook and write down the names of ten people that I want to either reach out to or check in with. A typical week might look something like this:

**Monday:** Use Google to search a competitor using the "-" exclusion query (Chapter 5). Check Google Images and web search to see what press outlets or blogs are featuring your competitor. Create a list of ten contacts, use Toofr to cross-check their e-mail address (or look them up on social media), create a personalized e-mail and make an offer to contribute. Boomerang followups to send one week later if no response is received.

**Wednesday:** Create a list of ten colleagues, clients, or partners that you worked with in the past. Share what you've been up to, check in to see what they've been up to, and ask if there's anything you can do to help them out. Boomerang followups to send one week later if no response is received.

**Friday:** Create a list of ten ubersuccessful entrepreneurs, CEOs, VIPs, celebrities, etc. If you feel intimidated to contact them, then you're on the right path. Mention how you're a huge fan of their work and invite them to be a guest on your mastermind call. Acknowledge that they are most certainly very busy, but have the chutzpah to reach out anyway. In virtually every area in life it's important to "punch above your weight." You never know what might happen.

Of course, you don't have to do it exactly this way - these are just a few examples. Focus on the type of contacts that are most vital to your own ventures, and fill up your list with those. The important thing is that you reach out to ten contacts on Monday, Wednesday, and Friday.

## Consistency for Results

Once you start to follow this schedule of contacting ten people every

Monday, Wednesday, and Friday, you will be proactively reaching out to 30 people every week, 120 per month, and 1,440 per year.

It might seem overly-simplistic, but simple works. Simple is beautiful.

Too many of us who are self-employed often occupy our time with "busy-work" that has nothing to do with making money. We occupy our time doing a thousand other things - from redesigning our website to research and reading - that we forget to talk to the people who matter most to our business.

Relationships = opportunities. Period. We have to get out in front of people and integrate the habit of outreach into our workflow. A solid outreach strategy allows us to grow our business ventures in a sustainable, organic way.

And yes - there will be times when you contact 10 new people, only to hear back from just one of them. When this happens, don't take it personally - it happens to the best of us.

Instead, look at it objectively - see it as a chance to improve. Perhaps your message was too long, it wasn't personalized enough, you didn't build enough of a relationship with the person beforehand, you didn't offer reciprocity, you didn't demonstrate enough value, or perhaps your offer wasn't strong enough.

The worst case scenario (which I hope you avoid) is to use the techniques in this book to contact 2-3 people, not hear back, and give up. Success doesn't come from isolated incidents; it stems from our habits. If you remember one thing from this book, remember this: ultimate success in any endeavor is the result of a consistent effort, and momentary instances of both success and failure are two sides of the same coin.

The real outcome that I hope you manifest from this book is not simply receiving a reply back from one or two people in an isolated instance, but rather that you adopt the skills and integrate these habits into your workflow. Focus more on building the skillset rather than the outcome.

If you create a habit, stick to a schedule, and keep consistent, I am completely confident that success will come.

# CASE STUDY: #1 BEST-SELLER IN AMAZON'S BUSINESS BOOK SECTION

This bonus chapter is a contribution by Nick Loper, founder of Side Hustle Nation, outlining the e-mail outreach tactics he used to promote his book, "Work Smarter," to an Amazon best-seller.

## My 659 Email Outreach Campaign

In this case study, Nick outlines the unique e-mail outreach tactics he's developed to market his book, explains which subject lines worked the best, and the apps he used to gain the most leverage during the campaign.

**Here are some of the hard numbers from the launch:**

- 20,215 free downloads

- 559 contributors

- 1247 paid downloads (so far)

- $427.83 in royalties the first week, and over $1400 in the first month

- 413 individual emails sent to contributors (183 responses, 44% response rate)

- 246 emails to featured companies sent (64 responses, 26% response rate)

- 334 new email subscribers (out of 580 visitors – 57% conversion)

- 200+ retweets and a social reach in the hundreds of thousands

- $108.43 in affiliate commission (explanation below)

- 70 5-star reviews

- 3 guest post opportunities, including one on EntrepreneurOnFire.com

- 2 guest appearances on large podcasts

- 2 free t-shirts, including this one from Buffer.

So without further ado, I present Nick!

# # Enter Nick

As a Kindle author during a free promo, your primary goal is to generate enough initial traction and downloads that your book starts to rank highly on Amazon's internal charts.

Reaching the top 5 in your category will virtually guarantee a strong download performance, so you should focus your efforts on getting enough volume to pump up your rank. Once you're there, Amazon will do the work for you. People will naturally discover it through the site; indeed, that's the beauty of tapping into the marketplace power of the world's largest store.

Here are the tactics I used to build that initial momentum.

## Marketing the Launch

The nature of my book, "Work Smarter: 500+ Online Resources Today's Top Entrepreneurs Use To Increase Productivity and Achieve Their Goals" with 500+ contributors and 350+ companies named, lent itself well to a massive email outreach campaign.

My efforts were broken up into 2 segments:

1. Contributors

2. Resources

The first step was gathering contact information, and I relied on a combination of Fancy Hands and my dedicated virtual assistant to help with this.

I spent an additional 25 Fancy Hands tasks building out the contact info (email addresses and "contact us" pages) in a Google Docs spreadsheet.

In many cases, I used Rapportive to guess/verify common email formats for these messages. In total, we were able to find reasonably reliable contact info for 659 different contributors and resources.

However, this was not without its own challenges. Rapportive temporarily blocked queries from my account 3 different times — probably for making too many database or API calls within a certain timeframe.

I spent 2 and a half days writing individual messages to everyone I could, and queued them up to send out Monday morning starting around 5am.

The tool I used to schedule the messages was Streak, a free Gmail extension. To write all the messages, I use Streak's "Snippets" feature, which lets you set up template emails, but tried to add in at least a line or two for personalization.

For example, if Rapportive showed me someone was in San Francisco, I'd mention I was based nearby. If they'd named a tool that was one of my favorites, I'd say so.

The reason to do it this way instead of in some sort of mail merge or mass mailing was to hopefully avoid the spam filters and get a better response rate. But honestly I had no idea if it would work or not.

**Subject line for contributors:** "I cited you as a contributor in my latest book project!"

**Subject line for resources:** "[Resource] is featured in my new book!"

I didn't get fancy and test different subject lines, but I just needed something compelling enough to get opened, coming from a complete stranger.

The interior of the message had 2 goals:

1. To generate downloads

2. To generate social shares

My hope was people would be curious enough about the project to go to Amazon and download a free copy. Each download helps push a book up the ranks.

## Click to Tweet

The next goal was social sharing, and I focused on Twitter because of the "click to tweet" tool. In each message, I included text that simply said:

"And if you think it's a cool project and want to share, here's a click-to-tweet link: http://ctt.ec/oAsf3"

With **Click to Tweet,** you can set a pre-written tweet for people to share. Here was mine: The idea was to make it as easy as possible for people to help spread the word, which in turn would generate more downloads.

One missed opportunity was not including a hashtag in the tweet. #Business #Entrepreneurship or even #Kindle could have led to wider discoverability, sharing, and possibly even becoming a trending topic.

By Sunday evening, I had nearly 400 messages ready to go out in the morning. I'd never attempted anything like this before and didn't know how reliable Streak would be or if my Gmail would get shut down.

(As a small hedge, I scheduled the messages to go out roughly a minute apart from each other, rather than blasting all of them out at 5am!)

I could barely sleep on Sunday night because I was nervous and excited to see what would happen on Monday morning! To be fair, I have nothing to compare it to, but in my mind the email campaign was a huge hit. It generated an excellent response rate (37% overall, and 44% among contributors).

More than 200 people shared the book on Twitter and Facebook, with a combined "reach" in the hundreds of thousands.

# CONCLUSION

That's it! Hopefully you got something out of this book, and picked up a few new tools, tricks, and techniques to help you become more productive and efficient with e-mail, as well as more persuasive and better equipped to promote and market yourself using e-mail.

If this is case, I'm thrilled.

I'd love it if you recommend this book to a friend, and I'd love it even more if you would take a minute or two to write a review on Amazon. Hopefully together, we can raise awareness for more intelligent and effective e-mailing!

Feel free to write to me with any questions or comments at: danny@openworldmag.com. I will personally respond to any messages from readers of this book.

And if you'd like more from me, please check out my other books on Amazon **on my author page,** or **visit my blog** for free content.

**Thanks for reading!**

*Danny Flood*

June 1, 2015

Bangkok, Thailand

# APPENDIX (RESOURCES)

Below is a list of links to each of the apps mentioned in this guide, in order of appearance:

| | |
|---|---|
| **Wisestamp** | **Key Rocket** |
| **Boomerang** | **Jing** |
| **Batched Inbox** | **Google Sites** |
| **Inbox Pause** | **Toofr** |
| **Streak** | **RecruitEm** |
| **Sidekick** | **Crowdfire** |
| **Rapportive** | **Twtrland** |
| **Full Contact** | **Triberr** |

*Scheduling Apps*

**Schedule Once**

**Calendly**

**Acuity Scheduling**

# ACKNOWLEDGEMENTS

A number of people helped to make this book what it is.

First, to all of the thought leaders who were my early mentors: such as Leil Lowndes, Robert Cialdini, Malcolm Gladwell, Lois Kelly, John Corcoran, Eric Von Sydow... and anyone else I've forgotten, thank you for helping me get a handle on the right principles of communication in the first place!

Special thank you to Chris Backe (One Weird Globe) and Vernon Foster II (Pod Parrot) for contributing early edits and suggestions to improve my manuscript. Thank you to Nick Loper (Side Hustle Nation), for offering your case study for this book and for always teaching me something new through your Udemy courses and value-packed blog.

Thank you to Scott Britton (Life-Long Learner) for introducing me to Toofr, and to Ryan Biddulph (Blogging from Paradise) and Meg Jerrard (Mapping Meagan) for teaching me how to use Triberr.

To all of my past and current clients, thank you for taking a chance on me and enabling me to do what I love to do.

To everyone who offered to act as a beta-reader to this book: Gregory Diehl, Katie Dowd, Manf Te, Sean Boyle, Jason Trick, Rick Noblett, Eric Williams, Leah Bell, Rob Tullis, and Mark Deal - thank you!

And lastly - my eternal gratitude to my late father, Jim Flood, for teaching me how to make others feel good and for showing me what it takes to succeed!

www.ingramcontent.com/pod-product-compliance
Lightning Source LLC
Chambersburg PA
CBHW072304200526
45168CB00014B/470